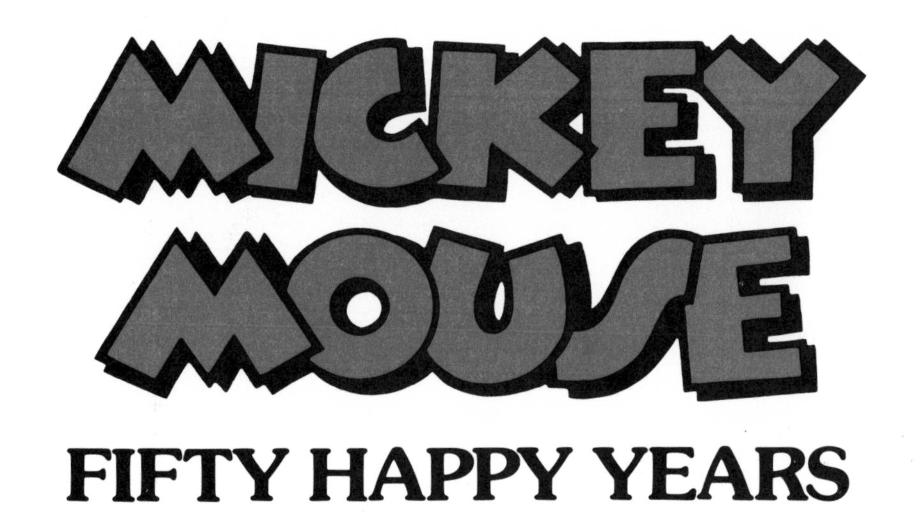
MICKEY
MOUSE
FIFTY HAPPY YEARS

MICKEY

FIFTY HAPPY YEARS

Edited by David Bain and Bruce Harris

Harmony Books/New York

H·A·R·M·O·N·Y B·O·O·K·S

Publisher: Bruce Harris
Editor: David Bain
Design: Ken Sansone
Production: Gene Conner, Murray Schwartz

Special thanks and a tip of the Harmony hat to our friends at Walt Disney Productions: Vince Jefferds, Wendall Mohler, Merrill Dean, Don MacLaughlin, Ed Quirk, Dave Smith, May Weigele, Manuel Gonzales, Floyd Gottfredson, and—especially—Merrie Lasky and Jeanette Kroger.

Harmony Books,
a division of Crown Publishers, Inc.,
One Park Avenue,
New York, New York 10016.

Printed in the United States of America.

Published simultaneously in Canada by General Publishing Company Limited.

Library of Congress Cataloging in Publication Data
Main entry under title:

Mickey Mouse: Fifty happy years.

Filmography: p. 252
Bibliography: p. 254
1. Mickey Mouse (Cartoon character) 2. Disney (Walt) Productions—History. I. Bain, David, 1949- II. Harris, Bruce S
NC1766.U52D55 1977 741.5'973 77-11076
ISBN: 0-517-52962-9

Contents

Introduction

by David Bain

Mickey Mouse . . . Mikki Hiiri . . . Miki Kuchi . . . Miguel Ratoncito . . . Topolino . . . Mikke Mus . . . Musse Pigg . . . Camondongo Mickey . . . El Ratón Mickey . . . El Ratón Miguelito: all names for a diminutive, pot bellied, slightly pear-shaped figure, with large ears and a knob of a nose. Usually found in short red pants with front buttons, and white gloves and yellow shoes, the creature is undoubtedly . . . a mouse. *Though firmly into middle age, he has changed only a little since his creation fifty years ago.*

There is something most appealing about this mouse—there is an intrinsic quality that reaches across time and through artificial, human-made barriers such as culture and nationality, to enter into the hardest of the hard-hearted and produce a smile.

*Duplicate our experiment: we took the Thirties cartoon title card of Mickey Mouse (head all aglow with sunbeams) and held it in front of an infant boy named Petersen, as he lay in his crib. As soon as the baby's eyes beheld the unfamiliar (only to him) face—*his face lit up. *He beamed. He smiled, and reached his hand out from the crib to touch the face that made him happy. There is something in Mickey Mouse's face that instantly evokes a response, even to an infant who's never seen him before.*

And all along the line—infants, savants, and savages——all respond. What is he? Who is he? Where did he come from?

To find out, we must begin by tracing the life and career of a midwestern commercial artist, until the two figures' paths cross, then continue side by side . . .

WALT DISNEY was born in Chicago on December 5, 1901, the next to youngest in a family of five children. His father, Elias Disney, was at different times in his life a building contractor, citrus grove operator, farmer, manager of a newspaper route, and jelly factory executive. His mother had taught school in Florida before marriage. When Walt was four, the family moved to Marceline, Missouri, where the elder Disney determined he could make a living at farming. This turned out to not be the case, so when Walt was eight, the family moved once more to Kansas City where Elias Disney purchased a newspaper route. In his later years, Walt Disney was fond of recalling the work he did on this paper route: getting up at 3:30 a.m. and trudging through snow drifts with his papers, going to school, then peddling more papers in the afternoon.

The young Disney showed an early skill at drawing and caricature; while on the farm he drew farm animals on the side of his father's barn, which prompted his aunt to give him a set of drawing materials. When he turned thirteen, he persuaded his father to enroll him in Saturday morning classes at the Kansas City Art Institute. This did not last long, however; Elias Disney decided to move back to Chicago and buy into a jelly factory. He and his wife and children left for Chicago, while Walt remained behind with relatives to finish out the school term. He was sixteen by then, and when summer vacation began, he got a job on the Santa Fe Railroad hawking candy to the passengers. In the fall of 1917 he joined his family, enrolled in high school, and began attending the Chicago Academy of Fine Arts three nights a week.

In 1917, his older brother Roy joined the Navy. Walt attempted to follow him, but was rejected because of his age. Instead, he joined a civilian ambulance unit, and soon thereafter found himself in France. The armistice had just been signed, so Disney spent much of his time chauffeuring Red Cross officials around and picking up spare change with his drawings.

"Walter E. Disney" stands in a snowy Chicago street, his face apparently set from a summer of hard work as a "candy butcher" on the Santa Fe R.R.

Returning to the United States in 1919, Disney eventually settled again in Kansas City, where he hoped to become a commercial artist. During a short term with one art firm, he met a young man named Ub Iwerks (of Dutch extraction), who would figure substantially in Disney's life later. When they were both laid off a few months later, they set up their own commercial art firm, but this enterprise proved to be short-lived. Soon Disney, and then Iwerks, abandoned their fledgling firm in favor of steadier employment with the Kansas City Film Ad Company. This, their first introduction to animation, had them producing crude stop-action commercials to be shown between features in local theaters.

Disney's friend from the early Kansas City days, Ub Iwerks, was the first animator of Mickey Mouse. He briefly left the Studio to create Flip the Frog, but soon returned. Besides animating, Iwerks had a hand in many of the Studio's innovative technological advances.

Disney became fascinated by animation, and soon was farming out his talents to a man named Newman—producing "Newman Laugh-O-Grams," humorous commentaries on contemporary events in Kansas City. When he had saved enough money, he left the Kansas City Film Ad Company to form his own "Laugh-O-Gram Films, Inc." and hired a group of artists (including Iwerks) to help produce them. They experimented for a while with various Nursery themes, before switching to a pilot for a series called "Alice Comedies," which featured a live child model cavorting among animated figures. Before they could go past the pilot film, their distributor went bankrupt, taking "Laugh-O-Gram" with it.

Disney was undaunted by his failures, but decided that perhaps a move to Hollywood was the answer. To finance the trip, he worked for a time as a freelance photographer for Pathé Newsreels, and also took pictures of children door to door for their parents. He slept on pillows in the defunct Laugh-O-Grams film studio. Arriving in the new film capital with the proverbial suit on his back, plus $40 and an "Alice's Wonderland" print, he lived with an uncle while unsuccessfully pounding the pavements in search of a job with a Hollywood studio. After two months of this, he signed with a New York distributor to revive the Alice comedies, and sent for his brother Roy who was living at the Sawtelle Veterans Hospital in Los Angeles. They began to produce the series in the rear of a real estate office.

Disney sent for Iwerks when it became apparent that Walt could not handle the animation duties alone, and a couple of women were hired to do the inking (one of whom, Lillian Bounds, would later become Disney's wife). The animation quality steadily improved, and success enabled them to buy a lot on Hyperion Avenue in Hollywood. In 1925, the "Disney Bros. Studio" had its first real home, and a new name—the Walt Disney Studio.

The Disneys gather in front of the first Disney Studio on Kingswell Ave. in Hollywood, ca. 1925: Lilly, Walt, Ruth (sister), Roy, Edna Disney.

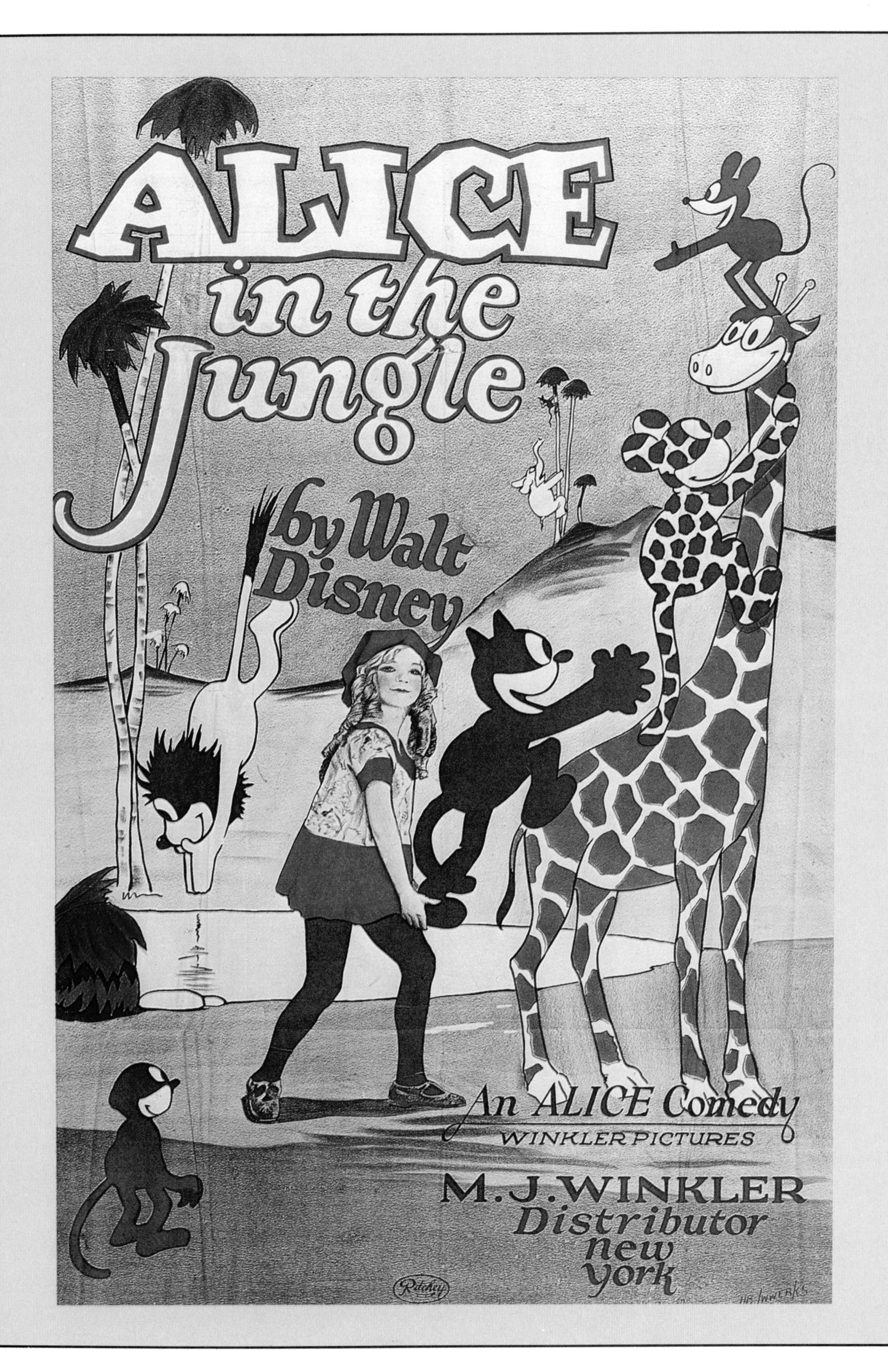
ALICE
in the
Jungle
by Walt
Disney
An ALICE Comedy
WINKLER PICTURES
M.J.WINKLER
Distributor
new
york
Ritchey
HB. IWWERKS

When Disney's distributor suggested trying a new character, the Disneys decided upon a rabbit. The name "Oswald" was picked out of a hat.

By 1927, the magic of Alice comedies had begun to fade, and the Disneys' distributor suggested they abandon them in favor of a totally animated series, which was called "Oswald the Lucky Rabbit." If it were not for a contractual flaw in the Disney agreement with their distributor in New York, Mickey Mouse might never have been born. As it was, the distributor, Charles Mintz, owned the character of Oswald, and when the series became successful he confronted Disney in N.Y. with a fait-accompli—accept a new contract at a lower price, or lose the character and his animators. As would be noted later, Mintz was the first of many to underestimate Disney. Disney, willing to lose his staff and begin anew, refused to negotiate further, and on the train ride back to Los Angeles (having cabled brother Roy some enigmatic words about everything being okay) he and his wife Lillian pondered creating another cartoon character to take Oswald's place. Disney recalled that during his Kansas City commercial art days his studio had been full of field mice—one of which proved to be especially tame. Disney trained the mouse to stay within a small circle by tapping it on the nose with a pencil every time it strayed. Once the character had been decided upon, only the name remained to be chosen. Disney's first choice was Mortimer, but his wife thought it too pretentious, so they settled on Mickey Mouse. The first scenario was concocted somewhere between Chicago and Los Angeles.

In 1927 Charles Lindbergh had made headlines for his celebrated New York to Paris solo flight. It seemed a natural to fashion a cartoon around a Lindbergh-like figure. When they arrived back in Hollywood, they went to work on "Plane Crazy," a barnyard caper inspired by midwestern barnstormers and especially Lucky Lindy. Mickey Mouse, complete with windswept thatch of hair, à la Lindbergh, courts Minnie Mouse by taking her up in his homemade plane. Numerous mishaps occur, including an hilarious cow chase in Mickey's low-flying plane, and Minnie's frenzied bailout from the plane, to escape Mickey's romantic advances.

The film was funny enough, as was its successor, "Gallopin' Gaucho" which featured Mickey and Minnie in a south of the border situation. "Gallopin' Gaucho" marked the introduction of the nefarious Pegleg Pete (minus, however, his wooden leg in this and a few subsequent films), a fat and evil cat who chases after Minnie and repeatedly attempts to make mincemeat out of Mickey.

Unfortunately, the East Coast distributors were unimpressed with his new characters. The nation was captivated by a cat named Felix, and the New York money men saw no profit in trying out a new animal in the theaters.

Right about this time, Warner Brothers was releasing an Al Jolson film, using their new Vitaphone process. "The Jazz Singer" was basically a silent film—subtitles and all—but the new sound process allowed them to augment the film with a few lines of dialogue and Jolson's songs.

The public was overjoyed with the novelty; the film industry was skeptical. But Disney, a tinkerer and always excited by innovative ideas, was thrilled by the possibility of producing a sound cartoon. He, Roy, Iwerks, and Lillian Disney brainstormed until they came up with the plot for "Steamboat Willie." One of their animators improvised an orchestration for the film—variations of "Turkey in the Straw," and "Steamboat Bill," and Disney came up with an elaborate method of synchronizing the animation and the music. Basically it called for an orchestra to play while watching a visual metronome provide the beat. The animators designed action to take place

"Steamboat Willie"

Sporting threads that could easily be accepted in today's fashions, the Studio poses with the star of "Alice in Cartoonland." Left to right: Ham Hamilton, Roy Disney, Hugh Harman, Walt Disney, Rudolf Ising, Ub Iwerks, and Walker Harman.

at the same timing. The wonderful quality of the film is dependent on the merging of the two effects.

"Steamboat Willie" was essentially a film about crew member Mickey's attempts to save passenger Minnie from Captain Pegleg Pete—and a sight/sound gag film. Mickey and Minnie cavort around the steamboat playing music on various animate and inanimate objects—using a cow's udders for a bagpipe, pots and pans as drums, a cow's teeth as xylophone, etc. The use of sound effects and musical score as the basis for all action in the film had never been done before. Even today the film is fascinating, but to audiences still unused to sound films it was nothing short of magic.

It is easy to see why the public would be so excited by a sound cartoon. A live picture such as "The Jazz Singer" would be novelty enough after years of silents—but Disney in his animation could show a steamboat funnel chugging in time with the soundtrack, and wring the oddest assortment of sounds from the steamboat's menagerie of passengers.

"Steamboat Willie" opened in New York at the Colony Theatre on November 18, 1928, and was an immediate success. The Disney Studio quickly moved to produce sound tracks for "Plane Crazy" and "Gallopin' Gaucho" and for a new Mickey Mouse cartoon entitled "The Barn Dance." Again, the work got to be too much for the tiny crew, so Disney wired to Kansas City for help in the person of Carl Stalling, a theater organist who had lent Disney money on several occasions. The latest addition was to prove as beneficial to Disney's fortunes as when Iwerks arrived, for the soundtracks began to be as sophisticated as the animation. The Mickey Mouse shorts became a national passion, and to accommodate the demand the studio added more personnel. It was around this time that they added a new series (at Carl Stalling's suggestion) called Silly Symphonies, which served to spread the Disney name. However, their lives were still near the poverty line, for Disney insisted on plowing all profits back into each new project.

The Mickey phenomenon grew. While the Disneys were in New York in 1930, someone offered them $300 to put Mickey's image on a school tablet. Disney accepted the offer, and a new sideline was added to his tiny empire—one that would help to keep the Studio afloat whenever Disney decided to embark upon a chancy new scheme. Kay Kamen, a New York merchandiser, was contracted to handle licensing of the Disney menagerie to toymakers everywhere. Soon kids all over the world were clamoring for Mickey Mouse toothbrushes, drinking glasses, combs, trains, watches, and an incredible assortment of toys and figurines that would number in the hundreds by 1935 and the thousands by 1960. It would be noted in the *Wall Street*

Overleaf: **A happy-looking poster advertised Mickey and Minnie in "The Whoopee Party," a 1932 film.**

A display case in the Disney Archives shows some of the character merchandise produced over the years.

JOSEPH M. SCHENCK
presents
WALT DISNEY'S
MICKEY MOUSE
IN "The WHOOPEE PARTY"
UNITED ARTISTS PICTURE

Journal that Mickey managed to pull two companies out of bankruptcy: the Lionel Train Corporation and the Ingersoll Watch Company. Manufacturers rushed out more products—all graced by the images of Mickey, Minnie, and the others who were beginning to overtake the mice in preeminence—Donald Duck, Pluto the Pup, Goofy, etc.

In 1930 King Features contacted the Studio for permission to run Mickey comic strips for newspapers—and soon another facet of the operation was under way, mostly under the direction of artist/writer Floyd Gottfredson. Those strips show as interesting an evolution of the figure, character, personality and fortunes of the Mouse as do the films. Beginning with a series of daily gags, Disney's staff soon switched to running stories that could go on for three or four months, at five strips per week. These long stories could be as entertaining as any of the short films, with the added feature that while they obviously lacked the movement present in the cartoon films, the personality of Mickey could develop over a year's time—he could talk more, do more, and stand for more than possible in a nine-minute cartoon film.

The stories' themes ranged from Mickey encountering a tribe of cannibals to a hair-raising adventure with an eccentric but cagey scientist with an antigravity device. Each story would run for months. Mickey would, in the end, capture the bad guys (or cats and dogs) and proceed wearily back home. Each time, he would no sooner step over the threshhold when faithful Minnie or another friend would enter with another important mission. Mickey often found himself during these years in the mid-Thirties running interference for the U.S. Secret Service or a similar glamorous organization. Of course, Pegleg Pete was his usual nemesis, as Pete seemed more than willing to sell out his country or his buddies to the highest bidders.

During their conflicts, highlights of language abound: "Why, yuh blasted little knob-nosed swab! I'll tear yuh apart," and "Mickey may be the apple of Minnie's eye, but he'll soon be applesauce," and "Listen, you blinkin, blasted, dumb-witted private," and a hunter's "Well bust my nose! A pelican t'practice on!"

Selected scenes from the heyday of Mickey's comics.

Mickey's evolution in the comic strips, 1930-present.

Of course, the characters continued to shuffle on and off the newspaper pages: Goofy (originally his name was Dippy Dawg), Donald, Mortimer Mouse (that name reappears throughout the Mickey history; in these cases, Mortimer was usually a rich uncle), and particularly slimy villain, Sylvester Shyster ("A crooked lawyer—the kind of guy who'd stick a knife in your back, then have you arrested for carrying concealed weapons."). It was precisely dialogue like this that calls to mind a troth between the Marx Brothers and Raymond Chandler, a mixture of high drama and low comedy. And like the Marx Brothers the earlier strips could not get through a day's feature with less than a pun a panel. Slapstick abounded throughout, but it was not the coarse slapstick of other comic features such as Herriman's Krazy Kat. It was mostly charm rather than cruelty, even in the cruder earlier days.

Mickey encountered the villainous Pegleg Pete in the Foreign Legion, aboard a smuggler's ship, and three thousand feet in the air. The little mouse was first to give his enemy a break, even though a few panels before he might have been triple-crossed by Pete. There was lots of violence in the strips, but it was the effortless violence of the period. Mickey got into more actual fistfights than most of us remember, and always demonstrated his pluckiness against overwhelming odds—fighting off hordes of bandits, pirates, hoodlums, wild west desperadoes, etc.

Opposite: **Mickey's three pals—Goofy, Donald Duck, and Pluto the Pup.**

Walt Disney, surrounded by a caseload of Mickey Mouse dolls. *Below:* Minnie Mouse, who stood faithfully by Mickey's side.

Throughout the Thirties the Disney Studio continued to turn out approximately eighteen Mickey Mouse cartoons a year. During this time, their sophistication grew as Mickey began to outgrow his barnyard beginnings. The Disney story department came up with idea after brilliant idea for the Mouse, and the public responded joyously. Douglas Fairbanks reported that during a safari his native bearers revolted until he showed them some Mickey Mouse cartoons—and they went back to work. Members of a South African tribe refused to buy cakes of soap unless they were embossed with the Mouse image—in the same manner as years earlier when they had refused coins that were not marked with the image of Queen Victoria. Mary Pickford visited the Disney Studio and posed for portraits with the Mouse, while it was reported in Britain that King George V insisted that all movies he attended feature Mickey Mouse. A similar demand was reported from President Roosevelt's White House. Even Madame Tussaud added Mickey Mouse to her wax museum.

In 1931 "Mickey's Orphans" was nominated for an Academy Award. This was the first of a long string of such recognition for Disney. Over the years, Mickey was nominated for five awards ("Mickey's Orphans," 1931; "Building a Building," 1933; "The Brave Little Tailor," 1938; "The Pointer," 1939; "Mickey and the Seal," 1948). In addition, Disney received a special "Oscar" for creating Mickey Mouse, in 1932.

What made him so enormously popular to such a huge international audience of all ages? This question has probably never been satisfactorily answered. Walt Disney himself could never adequately explain the Mouse Phenomenon, though he made many attempts, such as in this folksy interview from the Thirties:

Sometimes I've tried to figure out why Mickey appealed to the whole world. Everybody's tried to figure it out. So far as I know, nobody has. He's a pretty nice fellow who never does anybody any harm, who gets into scrapes through no fault of his own, but always manages to come up grinning. Why Mickey's even been faithful to one girl, Minnie, all his life. Mickey is so simple and uncomplicated, so easy to understand that you can't help liking him.

E.M. Forster pointed out once that "Mickey's great moments are moments of heroism." Certainly no other character in the history of film had so many roles in his or her career. Mickey was indeed a Renaissance Mouse. He could (and did) do anything, as Richard Schickel, film critic of *Life* magazine, would point out:

The Disney Studio on Hyperion Avenue, 1931. *Below:* Roy and Walt pose with Mickey and "Oscar"—after receiving a special Academy Award for creating Mickey Mouse.

The temporary solution to the problem of keeping Mickey fresh and amusing was to move him out of the sticks and into cosmopolitan environments and roles. The locales of his adventures throughout the 1930s ranged from the South Seas to the Alps to the deserts of Africa. He was, at various times, a gaucho, teamster, explorer, swimmer, cowboy, fireman, convict, pioneer, taxi driver, castaway, fisherman, cyclist, Arab, football player, inventor, jockey, storekeeper, camper, sailor, Gulliver, boxer, exterminator, skater, polo player, circus performer, plumber, chemist, magician, hunter, detective, clock cleaner, Hawaiian, carpenter, driver, trapper, whaler, tailor and Sorcerer's Apprentice.

Yes, Mickey could and did do everything, and easily outdistanced his contemporaries Felix the Cat, Krazy Kat, Oswald the Rabbit, Popeye the Sailor, Bugs Bunny, et al. In

Disney held a staff party in 1938 to celebrate the completion of *Snow White*. This charming illustration, by Ward Kimball, was on the cover of the party program, and marked the first use of pupils in Mickey's eyes.

This book proved to be enormously popular with children in the Thirties.

the heyday of his career—the 1930s—he surpassed all other characters. William Koslenko, writing in *The New Theatre* magazine, would write of the coarse and brutish ways of Popeye, and then go on to marvel "How versatile and refined, by comparison, is such a subject as Mickey Mouse, who can play the piano, ride a horse, conduct a band, fly an airplane, build a house, and do other constructive things with equal proficiency."

Another factor in the Mouse's favor was his easy access to the world. Not only were his films released at about one every four weeks in the Thirties, but sales of toys and other articles placed his smiling face before the public in every conceivable way. Mickey Mouse books, magazines, and—very prominently, comic books—were a constant presence in stores and news-stands around the world.

Towards the end of the decade, Disney began to plan for an extravaganza—a full-length animated feature, "Snow White." Its release marked, as Bosley Crowther would remark some thirty years later, the Continental Divide in Disney's work, as Disney would give less attention thereafter to the animated shorts that had been the Studio mainstay for a decade. But the shorts would continue; by now there were Donald Duck cartoons and Pluto cartoons and Goofy cartoons, and soon Chip and Dale would follow.

However, there was a change in the making of Mickey's personality. Perhaps, as has been related so many times, it was because of the avalanche of letters Disney got every time Mickey kicked someone in the pants. More likely, it was Disney's close identification with Mickey's personality (he often said, "there's a lot of the Mouse in me," and in fact did Mickey's voice in the films for nearly twenty years). Soon Mickey Mouse's personality began to evidence more maturity and less rambunctiousness. Some might point out that in the same manner that Disney took up polo as a pastime, so did Mickey in "Mickey's Polo Team." It was only a matter of time before Mickey joined his creator in the suburbs—which he did by the forties. He started to live in a suburban home and wear snap-brim hats, and comment upon Sinatra and later, rock and roll.

"The Sorcerer's Apprentice" was produced in 1938, but shelved for two years while work on *Fantasia* was completed.

It became apparent around this time (the late Thirties) that Mickey's popularity was slipping—giving way to that of Donald Duck, whose splenetic behavior got quicker laughs. To provide a comeback for Mickey, Disney chose an ancient fairy tale entitled "The Sorcerer's Apprentice." Leopold Stokowski readily agreed to conduct the Paul Dukas score. The project went so well that other segments were added, and the resulting feature film "Fantasia" marked a milestone in Disney's technological and creative career.

During World War Two, the studio output turned to help the war effort, and no Mickey Mouse cartoons were produced. However, the Allied Command code word during D-Day was "Mickey Mouse"—especially apropos, since the Nazis had called Mickey "the most miserable ideal ever revealed . . . mice are dirty."

Mickey totters on the brink of a giant-sized dining table, in a frantic attempt to dodge a menacing Giant, in *Fun and Fancy Free*.

In "The Simple Things," Mickey and Pluto try to get away for a relaxing vacation. Their peace of mind is interrupted by a squirting clam and some hungry (and larcenous) seagulls. This was Mickey's last film, and appeared in 1953.

In 1947, Disney reintroduced Mickey Mouse in "Fun and Fancy Free," a melange of animated shorts and live action. It received only lukewarm attention, though the Mickey segment, based on "Jack and the Beanstalk," was a superior offering. Mickey was in one short that year, and two in the following year. Mickey's physical presence in the animated film shorts remained pleasingly familiar. Perhaps his best film of the later period, was "Mickey and the Seal." This engaging tale concerned the hide-and-seek shenanigans of a small seal that takes a liking to Mickey and follows him home. An hilarious bathtub sequence (done many times previously by others, but not as effectively) involves seal-in-bathtub-without-Mickey's-knowledge. The film was nominated for an Academy Award.

ickey's last three appearances were in 1951, 1952 and 1953, respectively. The demand for animated short films had dried up. Moreover, by this time it was impossible to recoup production costs for any fully animated shorts. Disney would not accept less than top-quality animation, so the shorts just stopped appearing in theaters. The benignly cute Mickey Mouse, being poor competition to the wilder mania of

his colleagues Donald and Goofy (not to mention other studios' Tom and Jerry, Bugs Bunny and Roadrunner) was the first to go. Many in the industry were surprised that Disney stayed in the animated short film business as long as he did. The reason was that it kept his animators busy between major feature films. With the advent of Disney on television, their talents were needed for the new medium.

Also, it was becoming increasingly difficult to come up with plots and believable settings for a four-foot Mouse. The requisite shifts of proportion was hard for the Disney story department and animators to deal with. The animators' problem was that Mickey was too out of proportion with his environment. A mouse four feet tall was a very hard character to make believable. The story people had many limitations too.

So Mickey became the ambassador for Walt Disney Productions. Whenever the studio decided to be innovative Mickey was on hand to guide the public to the next Disney entertainment. His visage could still be had on hundreds of pieces of merchandise. When Walt Disney built his theme park at Anaheim in 1955, Mickey was chosen to be the official host.

Perhaps Mickey's role on television as master of ceremonies was the best one left to him. In 1955, Disney entered the syndicated television market with his "Mickey Mouse Club"—with Mickey as master of ceremonies. The variety- format show starred a handful of California kids who sang and danced their way into millions of homes for a three-

Above: **The Mickey Mouse Club was an extraordinarily popular television show in the mid-Fifties, and caused millions of American kids to buy and wear the official Mickey Mouse Club cap *(below)*.**
Opposite page: **There will always be a Mickey Mouse figure in a Disney theme park. Here he rides triumphantly in a Disneyland parade.**

Mickey appeared occasionally on "Walt Disney Presents." Here he and Walt look at Mickey's memory album.

year period. Each day featured a revived cartoon from the Disney archives, and millions of children were thereby introduced to the likes of Mickey and Minnie Mouse and their friends. On the "Mickey Mouse Club" he would one day glide in on a magic carpet, saunter in another day dressed in chaps and cowboy hat. He seemed his old folksy, somewhat shy and bemused self.

Running also at this time was "Disneyland," later called "Walt Disney Presents" and "The Wonderful World of Color." Mickey appeared sporadically in these shows; his recycled cartoons were featured regularly. On the Disney variety show he could often be found perched on Disney's desk, talking with Walt. In early 1977, a new Mickey Mouse Club was released for television, and syndicated nationally. So, as Mickey reaches his fiftieth year, he continues before the national (and international) audience, albeit in a less strenuous manner than in the early days.

There is really no answer to the question of "what was (is, will be) so special about Mickey Mouse." He was, after all, a likeable character, and made friends extraordinarily easily. But there is some special quality that surpasses mere charisma (something that surprised and confounded even his creator). Mickey Mouse knew no nationality or creed; he was truly universal. As he will continue to be, for the next fifty years, and thereafter.

In the shadow of Mickey: Walt Disney poses for the Studio photographer in the mid-Thirties.

MICKEY
MOUSE
FIFTY HAPPY YEARS

Steamboat Willie, 1928

Although "Steamboat Willie" was the third completed Mickey Mouse cartoon, it was released first, for it had something the other two shorts —and, for that matter, any others—did not have: a synchronized sound track. Complete with orchestra, cow bells, whistles, whoops and snorts, "Willie" was the story of how first mate Mickey saves Minnie Mouse from the nefarious Captain Peg-Leg Pete. It was a situation that was to be repeated many times, always to the audience's delight.

Plane Crazy, 1928

The scenario for "Plane Crazy" was concocted on a cross country train trip, by Walt and Lillian Disney. Their new character evidences his Mickey ingenuity very early on, as he goes about plane construction with a cheery disregard for the laws of nature and scientific method. "Plane Crazy" was the first Mickey Mouse cartoon, though it was not publicly released until after "Steamboat Willie."

Construction is already in full swing at the aircraft factory,

where an amazing aircraft with a rather strange engine is being built,

destined to be a landmark in aviation technology.

And our hero, Mickey Mouse, prepares himself for his destiny

as super pilot, licking his fingers

as he turns over the pages in his flying instruction book.

(A nasty habit!) Suddenly he spots a picture

of the biggest hero of them all—

CHARLES LINDBERGH, King of the Air, the "Lone Eagle" himself!

— Do I look like him?
Not much, I guess,

My face sure isn't
known as a pilot.

But if I looked like Lindbergh,
everyone would *know* I was an ace.

I've got it! His hair is
is sorta messed up.

If I mess mine up, NOBODY
could tell us apart! —

The great day has dawned . . .
the plane is finished,

and the Dachshund motor
is waiting on the runway.

But first he's steps
for Pilot Mickey

— Goodbye, dear friends.
I'm off to the wild blue yonder —

Well, actually I'm going
around the world. —

Everything ready? Okay,
Docksy. Climb in

and get ready to spin the propeller.
Take it easy now —

There's a lot of you
to get in there!

And Dachshund grabs the
back of the propeller

in his teeth and
spins like a top,

as Piglet winds him up by
cranking the propeller.

When the propeller starts to whir,
Piglet is as surprised

as the pilot! The
plane takes off —

but not into the
wild blue yonder.

It bucks and crawls.
It whips and bumps.

It's up! It's down!
It twists and turns!

Mickey hangs onto the stick
for dear life,

and finally, with great courage,
gets the plane headed straight.

But straight for what?
Oh, boy! The controls won't work,

and here comes a tree that doesn't
have the decency to step aside!

WHAM! The tree, the plane, and
Mickey all see stars.

What a mess! Everything is smashed
to smithereens, and Dachshund,

who was doing duty as the engine,
crawls out and vanishes.

Mickey, catapulted out of
the plane across the field,

staggers to his feet, and
limps away dejectedly.

Then he stops short. What's this?
Could it be . . . . ? It *could!*

An old Tin Lizzie, with all the
parts *any* plane designer needs.

So here we go again.
— Let's see, now. We'll need

this for the wings. If we
move that over there,

and prop up the front
a little bit,

and use the old propeller that
hit the ground when I did,

I don't see why it shouldn't
fly like a bird!

Oops! I forgot to pull
out the tail parts . . .

Tail parts? What *will* I use
for a tail? Well, well!

A turkey, as I live and
breath. I'm sure he'd

sacrifice it for the sake
of science. — YANK.

Now the job is done.
The results are fantastic.

A streamlined plane; light as
a feather — or feathers.

"Now *that* looks like a *real*
plane, Mickey," says Minnie,

"Minnie, you're an angel!
A real thoughtful kid.

"and I've brought you
a horseshoe for good luck.

This flight will have to
be a success!"

Why don't you come along?
We'll have a ball!"

In she hops, as
excited as Mickey.

The daredevil pilot is
getting ready for take-off.

The propeller spins;
the ship leaps forward

on its way, raising
a cloud of dust.

It happened so fast that the
pilot lands on the ground,

and poor Minnie is all
alone in the airplane,

yelling at the top of her lungs,
as the plane heads straight

for Caroline, the cow,
who sees it coming

and takes off like an
antelope (a distant cousin).

But the aircraft pursues
relentlessly, closing in on her.

Don't look back, Caroline
don't . . . . look . . . . back!

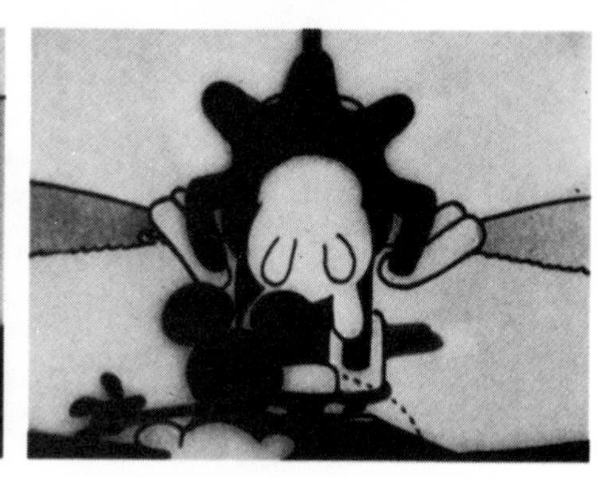

The cow that jumped
over the moon couldn't

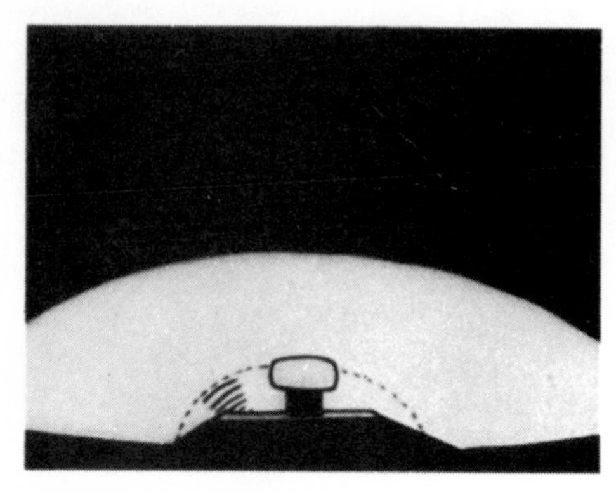

have moved *this* fast.
The plane points up . . .

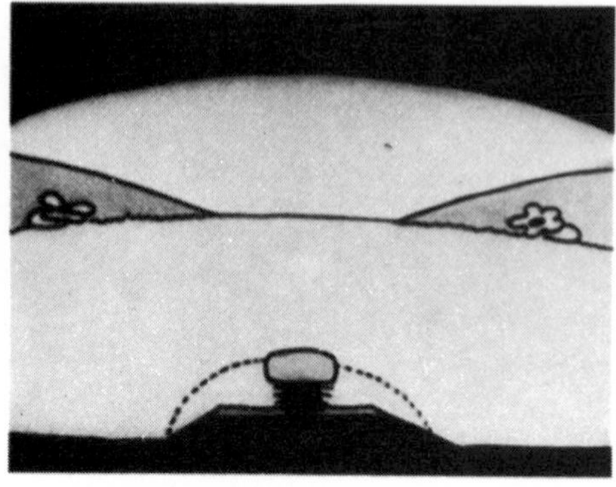

no, it points down. And
Minnie, looking ahead,

sees that Caroline seems to
have vanished. But she hasn't.

She grabbed hold of the tail
as the plane swooped over her,

and Mickey, with a jump,
clutches her by the udder.

He is udderly surprised, too,
when he's almost drowned

in a milk bath. He
lets go, and now

Minnie and Caroline get
even more panicky.

Don't worry, girls. Mickey
is up and at 'em again.

He races after the plane, gives a great
leap, and grabs Caroline's tail.

WHOMP! Caroline lands on the ground,
flattening Mickey like a pancake.

They get themselves collected, and
the dauntless Mouse

uses Caroline as a
mount. "Run! Run!"

"Faster! Faster! We'll catch it."
But Caroline's out of breath.

So Mickey runs down her back
and yanks her tail.

Her long neck snaps forward
like a rubber band.

Mickey races along toward the
rear end of the plane, and

leaps aboard in the
twinkling of an eye.

Jumping over Minnie, he makes it to the pilot's seat,

takes hold of the controls, and CRAACK . . .

the control stick breaks in two. And now

the plane really takes off in whirls and loops.

Minnie clutches Mickey's pants in terror.

Oh, Golly! Look what's ahead! A church steeple!

But it's smarter than the tree. It just folds up,

so our hero and heroine are still with us.

"Darling Minnie, everything is O.K. now. Why don't you

give this ace pilot a big hug and kiss?"

"What are you waiting for, my love? Don't you want to kiss me?"

"Kiss you! After what I've been through today?

Fat chance." "I don't give up *that* easy . . . "

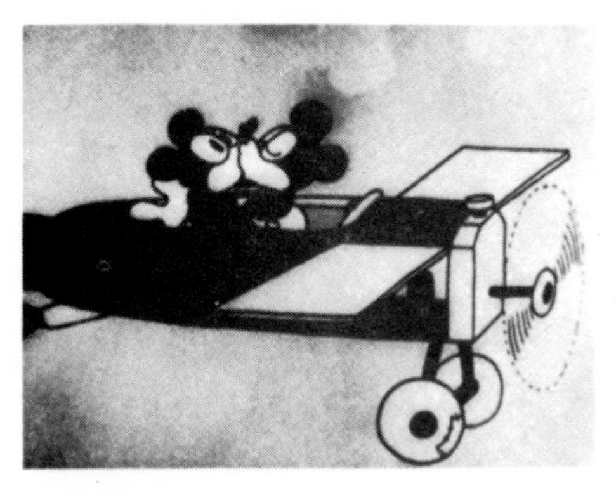

and Mickey gives Minnie a smacking kiss.

"Think you can get away with it, do you? Take this . . .

. . . and that. That'll make you see stars!"

"And now, my one-time friend, so long . . . . I'm leaving this crazy plane and its stupid pilot."

"Watch out! Where do you think you're going? We're in the air, or didn't you know?"

But Minnie has jumped and is going down in an awful hurry

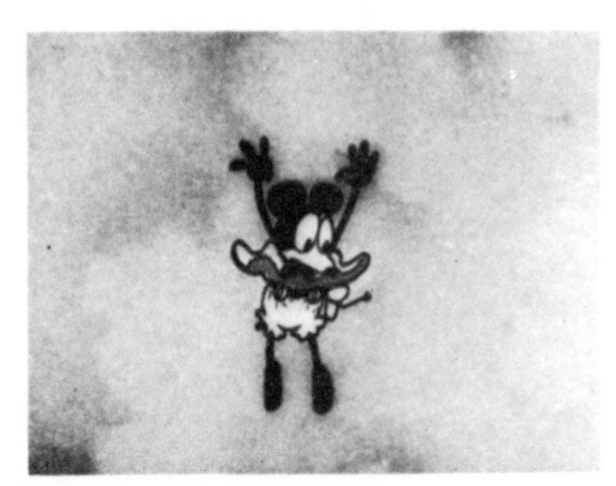

when she decides she'd better do something fast.

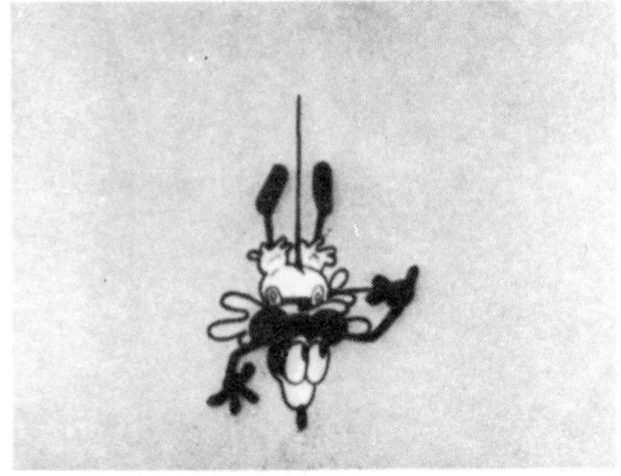

So she pulls a string on her panties and PRESTO!

They've turned into a parachute

that gets bigger and bigger and
wafts her gently to earth,

while poor Mickey, hanging
onto the plane's tail,

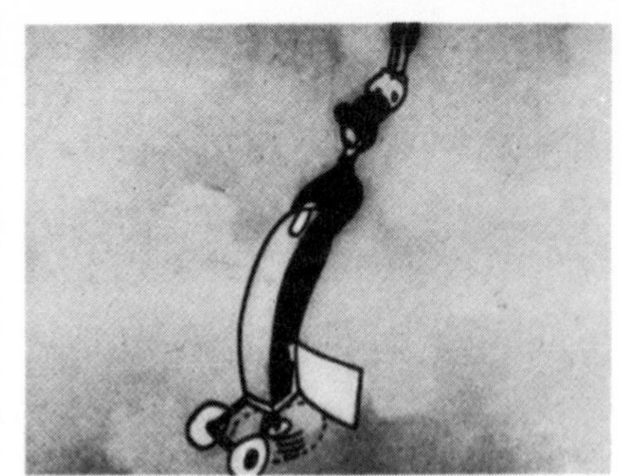

is headed down
in a nose-dive.

CRASH . . . BANG . . . .
Oh, Mickey!

But thanks to his lucky
horseshoe, he's okay.

Now Minnie lands
next to our hero,

with panties that are
considerably stretched.

She tries to yank
them up, and Mickey

begins to howl with laughter.
Minnie, insulted, stalks off. . .

as Mickey flings the horseshoe,
only to have it boomerang.

The adventure has come to
an end. . . . Mickey's out cold,

dreaming of how to improve
his *next* airplane.

Gallopin' Gaucho, 1928

The second Mickey Mouse cartoon, "Gallopin' Gaucho" was originally a silent. It remained unreleased until the success of "Steamboat Willie" made it possible to add a soundtrack. This was Mickey's first swashbuckling role, and he rescued Minnie with great finesse.

Mickey's Orphans, 1931

Mickey and Minnie host a gala Christmas bash for a group of tiny kittens. The orphans' mischievous natures lead to mayhem, though only Pluto seems to be upset about the state of affairs: he plainly does not enjoy being used as a swing *(page 50)*, but his expression *(page 51)* cannot be read!

Mickey in Arabia, 1932

Mickey and Minnie journey to exotic Arabia in this film, and encounter some pretty exotic characters. Minnie almost winds up in a seedy Sultan's harem, but Mickey comes to the rescue.

Touchdown Mickey, 1932

In this rollicking football thriller, a hodgepodge team of puny players battle a frighteningly professional group of thugs. Mickey scores a fantastic goal by plunging beneath the gridiron and burrowing to victory between the goal posts.

RADIO BOX

RADIO BOX

Mickey's Nightmare, 1932

Mickey dreams of an army of toddlers, who arrive via storks. The mayhem in this film is most inventive, as the little mice take over (and nearly destroy) Mickey's home. Luckily, it was only a dream.

Mickey's Gala Premiere, 1933

In this marvelous film, Mickey and Minnie are the guests of honor at Grauman's Chinese Theater. Their admirers are legion, as we see. *Below:* Stan Laurel and Oliver Hardy; Marie Dressler, Wallace Beery, and Lionel Barrymore in his Rasputin character. *Opposite page:* The Keystone Kops (including Ben Turpin, Ford Sterling, Harry Langdon, and Chester Conklin); Greta Garbo; Bela "Dracula" Lugosi, Frederic "Dr. Jekyll" March, and Boris "Frankenstein" Karloff; Maurice Chevalier and Eddie Cantor; Marie Dressler, Joe E. Brown, Cantor, Stan & Ollie, and Jimmy Durante; and Harold Lloyd and Charlie Chaplin himself! What a party! Oh—it turns out to be only a dream.

WDM

The Band Concert, 1935

The first Mickey Mouse cartoon in color, this film features Mickey as leader of a concert band, and Donald Duck as a persistent popcorn hawker. Mickey desperately tries to conduct his band through "The William Tell Overture" in the face of Donald's distractions.

Mickey made several appearances in films done by studios other than Disney's, including *Hollywood Party* in 1934, starring stage star Marilyn Miller. When Hal Roach produced his Laurel and Hardy extravaganza *Babes in Toyland (above)*, he employed not only Mickey but The Three Little Pigs. Here, Mickey and the Cat in the Fiddle worry over the plight of Tom-Tom the Piper's Son, who was wrongly accused of pig-stealing. Later in the picture, Mickey played a decisive role in the battle against the Bogeymen and their leader Barnaby—by boarding a miniature blimp and bombing the opposing army with firecrackers before parachuting to safety.

Mickey's Kangaroo, 1935

Around the same time that a New York paperback publisher commissioned the Disney Studio to create a kangaroo emblem for their line of books, the animation department produced "Mickey's Kangaroo," who bore a striking resemblance to the publisher's "Gertrude." In this cartoon, Mickey and Pluto are visited by a pair of boxing kangaroos (one of whom rides in the larger one's pocket). Pluto is understandably dismayed by these strange animals.

The Mad Doctor, 1933

In "The Mad Doctor" Mickey takes a spine-tingling trip through a haunted laboratory. At one point, he lights a match to find his way through the darkness, only to have a skeleton appear and blow out the match. Mickey winds up tied to an operating table, surrounded by formidable-looking scientific equipment. Nevertheless, he escapes.

As his fame begins to spread, Mickey stands in the Disney office, surrounded by trophies, in this publicity photograph. When *American Heritage* used this on their cover in 1968, they captioned it, "The squeak heard round the world."

Thru the Mirror, 1936

Lewis Carroll's stories were a constant fascination for Disney. One of his earliest series was "Alice in Cartoonland," and in 1951 he released his animated musical feature *Alice in Wonderland.* "Thru the Mirror" was a natural vehicle for Mickey and delightfully surreal.

Mickey's Rival, 1936

"Mickey's Rival" combined many marvelous elements: Mickey's stoic good manners in the face of his slick rival's harassment; a helpful jalopy; and a dramatic bullfight.

What can be better than a picnic in the open air on a beautiful spring day? It even excites the curiosity (and appetites)

of the little inhabitants of the wood. Pretty Minnie is setting the table . . . or tablecloth. But is she really all by herself?

No! Do you think she'd go on a picnic without her inseparable Mickey Mouse? Here he is, and there's no way he can get in trouble *here*.

How peaceful it is! How serene! But the peace is short-lived. The still air of the countryside is shaken by a thunderous noise. It sounds like . . .

an automobile! A powerful, custom-made car that is heading straight for Minnie and Mickey Mouse, as though it were on the speedway!

"Oh! It's him! How *nice* of him to come and look us up here!" cries Minnie, as she recognizes the reckless driver . . . and holds onto her hat.

WHOOSH! Good-bye, picnic! Caught in the slipstream, the picnic lunch scatters every-where . . . plates, rolls, bottles,

and other tidbits bombard poor Mickey, who is stunned. "What's going on? There goes my pie! Our whole lunch!"

WHOOSH! Women and children first . . . and where does that leave the mice? I can see the chicken, but Minnie . . . where are YOU???

SCREECH! The automobile skids to a stop, leaving tire tracks on the meadow and removing about a ton of turf.

What a slicker *he* is! "Let's find a convenient place to park my twelve cylinders . . . in the shade, if possible . . . ."

There? Whadd'ya mean *there*? Under that tree . . . is the only shade around. But that's where Mickey's old jalopy is parked. No room there.

Are you kidding? POOF!! POOOF!!! It's no good blowing your horn. You just can't argue with some characters.

Wow! Not even the most easy-going driving instructor would let *that* get by in a parking test.

He's as athletic as he is sharp. Some people will do anything to attract attention . . . Wouldn't it be simplest just to open the door and get out?

But Mortimer apparently doesn't even know that a car has doors. Make way there!

"Oh, Mortimer! What good wind brings you here?" "An enchanted one, my lovely little lady. How are you?"

"Oh! very well . . . but what are you doing??" "Allow me, dear Minnie, to pay homage to your (SMACK!) incomparable beauty!"

"Come now, silly boy! I want to introduce you to my fian . . . well, to a friend of mine. . . . He'll be delighted to meet you!"

"MICKEY! Yo-hoo! Come here! I've such a *nice* surprise! MICKIEEEE! Where has that boy hidden himself?"

—Cough? PHEW! What's she mean "Where have I hidden myself?" Where did she think her "nice surprise" catapulted me?

The pie *is* a bit sticky, isn't it? Poor Mickie Mouse . . . but if you'd eaten it, you'd be still worse off!

"It looks pretty indigestible, if you ask me. But talking of looks, who is that lovely blonde girl?"
"That's it, try to be funny!"

"Come here, Mortimer, and please excuse Mickey's behavior. He doesn't know what good manners mean. He's not like you!"

"Mickey! Meet Mortimer! Just think: he drove all the way from the city to keep us company. Isn't that *adorable*?"

"Hey, there, old man! Don't you think you're a bit too big to fool around in short pants?"
"I wear whatever I like!"

"Aw, come on. Don't be so sensitive. Forget I said it. I didn't mean anything. . . . Friends, okay? Give me some skin!"

"Eh, you're pretty flabby, you know! Give it a bit of muscle! Shake, like a man!"
"If you say so. . . . " CRACK! TLACK!

"What the dickens is *that*?"
"Say, man, you're not a mouse! You're a Hercules! Hahahaha!"

"A false arm! I might have known you'd pull a silly practical joke like that!
Just a silly, false, inoffensive arm. . . . "

ZONK! BANG! Silly, maybe, but inoffensive, no! At least, not by the look that's on your face.

HAR! HAR! "What a laugh! I'll get a belly ache if I laugh any more!
What a dope! He fell for it!"

"You're the dope, you big snout! Just try it again. . . . " "Who d'you think you are, kid? You don't mean to tell me

that it really got to you? Because, see here, I can take something, too, one of these pretty buttons, for example. . . . "

"Ah! that riled you, didn't it! Pity there isn't a mirror handy, so's you could see your face! It's a real beaut!"

"I'll give you beaut, you bum! Give me back my button this minute, or I'll shut
that grinning trap of yours! Grrrr. . . . "

"What a to-do, just for an imitation gold button! I'd better take another one,
so that you stay symmetrical!"

"See here, Sharpie! If we're talking buttons, I'll grab these two. . . .
Then what'll. . . . Oops!"

"Surprised, Mickey? Didn't you know?
That's the way they sew buttons on nowadays!"
"Why use such a stupid kind of thread?"

ZACK! ZRISSS! "Very special. . . .
ultraspecial thread, kid!
ZACK! ZICK! "HELP! HELP!"

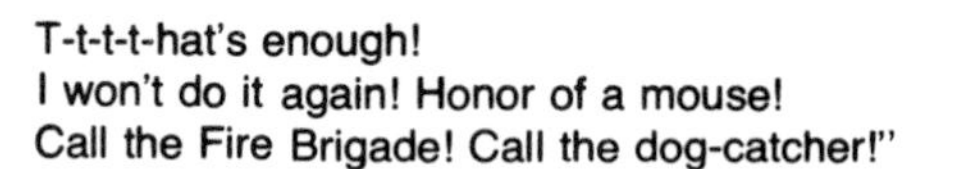

T-t-t-hat's enough!
I won't do it again! Honor of a mouse!
Call the Fire Brigade! Call the dog-catcher!"

"What are you laughing for, you jerk? If it hadn't been for that thunderbolt, you'd be laughing out of the other side of your face!"

"Hear that, folks?? Thunderbolt, he says! When did they let you out alone, kid? Didn't anybody ever tell you about high-charged batteries?"

If Mickey Mouse is weeping with rage, his jalopy isn't laughing, either! The poor thing is smashed between the sports car and a very solid tree.

It keeps blowing its horn, heaving, pushing, using all the strength of its 1½ HP, and finally it manages to get free.

—Now I'll show you, you custom-made nothing! I'm a historic model, you snooty no-good!

BEEP! BEEP! Wild honking of horn. Haughty with its twelve cylinders, the custom-made car doesn't even bother to turn around.

Then, all of a sudden . . . HEEK HONK! HEEK HONK! That racket could give somebody a heart attack.

—Shiver my cylinders! That must be an armored tank in disguise! I'd better stay clear of it!

Panic to the left (Mickey's jalopy); fury to the right (Mickey himself). Mortimer and Minnie in the middle,

happy as clams. Mortimer is eating as if there was no tomorrow. "What's this, chicken?"

GNAW! GNAW! SLURP! GNAW! GNAW! "I'm crazy about roast chicken! And this one couldn't be better."

"And what about some cookies Mickey? Watch out, you're getting your paw wet! If Mortimer notices, he'll make fun of you again!"

But you needn't worry, Mickey; what with gnawing and slurping, the Sharpie is too busy to notice that you're dunking your cookies.

What now? A concert with chicken bones? CLICK CLACK! Seems as though the Sharpie knows all the parlor tricks, too!

BLOW! SNORT! A sound from the field interrupts the noisy concert. "Holy cats, what's that? Look, Mortimer, will you?"

Mortimer looks. He sees in the distance a bull and a stout fence (which is much nearer). SNORT! SNORT! BELLOW!

Not a very comforting sight!—But when did you people last look at yourselves in the mirror? I'm a bull! A FIERCE bull.—

"Now let's have some fun, Minnie! Want to see a genuine bull fight? Give me the tablecloth. . . . "

SWOOSH! How about that? Now a man can't even dunk his cookies in peace!

SPLOSH! "Well . . . you've done your dunking, Mickey! But I don't expect that's the way you prefer to do it."

"How true! But tell me something: who are you supposed to be with? Me or that jerk?" "With you, of course! But now . . . let's watch!"

"Adios, Minnie! Mortimer, the Handsomest Sharpie and Greatest Bull-Fighter in the world, will dedicate this bull to you!"

SNORT! BELLOW! SBUFF! "Hey, there, bull! Come and charge my red cloak! I dare you! But don't forget

to hit the fence first! Vamos! Show Señorita Minnie what a brave bull you are (and what a brave matador I am, incidentally!)."

POW! POW! BANG! BING! "Olé! What timing! I don't like to boast, but there's no doubt I'd have been an ace matador, if I'd been born in Spain! Poor old bull, he took that hard. He didn't expect me to play a trick like that on him!

CLAP! CLAP! CLAP! "Minnie, don't be too carried away. For an athletic type like me, that was nothing!"

"Isn't he *marvellous*?! What a hero! And what a fascinating man! Don't you think so, Mickey?" "I'm off. . . . If I don't go, I'll explode!"

"But, Mickey . . . where are you going? *Why* are you going? You're not . . ." "I am what I am, and I'm going. Enjoy yourself!"

"Oh! I get it! Mr. Mickey Mouse is jealous! Mr. Mickey Mouse can't stand by and see that there are people smarter than him! Tee-hee!"

—Women! I'll never understand them! How can she get all excited over that cheap . . . no-good . . . Bah!

Mortimer seems very pleased with himself. He's just had an idea. "The ugly mug has disappeared. The moment is ripe, Mortimer. Get moving."

"Minnie darling, would you like me to repeat that trick you admired so much? I'll settle this bull's hash once and for nothing!" Ulp!—What idiot went and opened that gate? Didn't they know I've got heart trouble?!

MUU! SNORT! Don't let me down, legs! If he catches me, it's all over! How did I get into this mess?"

GALLOP! GALLOP! GALLOP! Anyone who plays with fire . . . is apt to get burnt. And anyone who fools with bulls, is likely to get gored!

—May the flower on my new hat wither if I'm not scared to death! "Mortimer, do something! DO SOMETHING QUICK!"

"Aren't I doing something already? I'm hightailing it to safety! Don't waste my time, baby! I've got an important date in town!"

"Filthy coward! Deceiver of innocent maidens! Keep out of my way from now on, d'you hear . . . unless you . . ."

"No fear of that, baby . . . I don't think I'll be seeing you around anymore! 'Bye-bye! Give my regards to the bull and your boy friend,

the Mouse! Pity I have to take off in such a hurry! It's been such a pleasant day!" ZOOM!!!!

"It sounds like a train passing by! Odd . . . I don't remember seeing any railroad tracks around here!"

CLOP! CLOP! GALLOP! SNORT! SNORT! BELLOW! If this isn't a super-express heading this way, will you tell me what it is?

"It's . . . the . . . b-b-b-b-ull!! If I have a guardian angel, I need you now! Heavens, how ugly he is! HELPPP!"

SNORT.—What game are we playing? First you disturb me in my field and now you insult me!! SNORT! SNORT!

"MICKEY! MICKEY! Help me! Save me! I'll forgive you for everything, but save me!" (Too bad she can't see where she's going!)

—It's Minnie in real trouble! I'll have to forget I'm angry and try to help her! "Minnie, I'm coming!"

"Step on it, then! I can't see a thing but I can feel breath burning all down my back!"

"I'm not Super Mouse, you know! I need at least a few frames to start running!" Ready? OFF!

Will the raging bull overtake poor Minnie? Will the heroic Mouse head him off in time? Can you stand the excitement?

"Give me that tail!" SHRIEK! "Got you, you overgrown calf, you! You're through playing the heavy in front of girls! Fight me . . . like a man!"

Challenge a bull and you're asking for it. "When I said, 'Come here and fight!' I didn't mean it *this* way! Look out! I'm here, too, you know!"

KERPLONKK! Poor Mickey! (When you think just how much a bull weighs!) Right: how much *does* a bull weigh? Now, let's see:

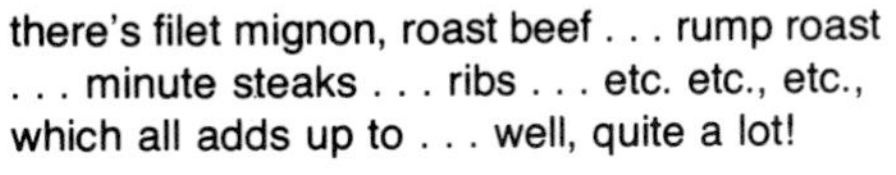

there's filet mignon, roast beef . . . rump roast . . . minute steaks . . . ribs . . . etc. etc., etc., which all adds up to . . . well, quite a lot!

"A lot! You can say that again! I'm telling you!" (Those words are Mickey's, but his voice sounds quite suffocated), as with

tremendous difficulty, he manages to struggle out from underneath the enormous rump and take the offensive.

What you're looking at is not a commercial for a paste to whiten the teeth whiter than white . . . because

not even bleach will do that. No, this is a "live" action scene. You ask the bull, if you don't believe us. SNAP!

MOOO! AAAAHI! Mice teeth in ox-tail! Doesn't sound very tasty. Actually it's a painful fact!

Painful for the bull, who, obeying the law which says the bigger they are the harder they fall, falls down again after it had got up. Run, Mickey!

BOING! He runs just in time to keep himself from being flattened again. Taking advantage of the bull's momentary,

stunned condition, Mickey's only concern is to get Minnie into safety. "Quick, climb up! The bull is coming to!"

You can say that again! CLOPPETTY CLOP-PETTY CLOPPETTY! SNORT! Enraged at being thrown by a mouse, the bull is

determined to repay that bite with his horns. "I'd better beat it . . . or there could be a serious misunderstanding!"

BUMP! BUMP! Saved by a hair! In blind fury, the bull-dozing bull hits the tree head on!

What tree is that? The one Minnie has climbed! And it's really the girl that the bull is after, thinking she's fruit hanging up there!

To distract the ferocious beast's attention and save his sweetheart, Mickey makes a heroic decision: to turn matador!

The gantlet is thrown down . . . the challenge accepted! BELLOW! SNORT! This'll be real fireworks . . . and there's no fence this time!

Olé! Mickey whips a mean cape . . . er . . . tablecloth . . . and he hasn't even taken a correspondence course in bull-fighting.

Great timing! Great dodge! But somehow I have a very uncomfortable feeling that

the next phase will leave something to be desired. Carried away by his turn, the matador gets tangled up

in his red cloak. Nasty state of affairs! When you need your legs, it's not very pleasant to find them . . .

(and the rest of you) wrapped up like a mummy! Hopping and skipping, Mickey Mouse tries to run for it . . . .

Desperate, sure, because the bull is gaining on him. Give it all you've got, Mickey! You've got to get out of this alive!

"Get out of it? You make it sound so easy! As if there were lots of things I could do . . . H'm . . . "

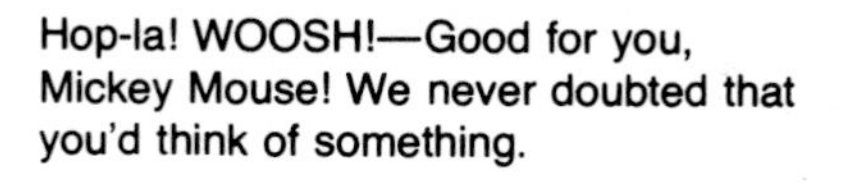

Hop-la! WOOSH!—Good for you, Mickey Mouse! We never doubted that you'd think of something.

CRACK! BUMP! Tsk, tsk! Didn't you know that boughs sometimes break? "Sure, but why *this* one?"

Did you ever hear of a blue funk!!? Wrapped like parcel post (and not even stamped) . . . and with . . . ULP! . . .

a bull in fighting trim at your heels!
Forgive me if I don't stick around . . .
but I'm rather pressed for time!

Poor Mickey! Who can help him?
—I can, I can! I can't stand by
and see him clobbered!

He's always fed me with lots
of oil and gas . . . with the highest
octane rating! Charge! PUFF! PUFF!

Baring its teeth and rumbling,
the brave jalopy
takes after the bull!

Scooping him up on its hood, it sweeps
him a respectable distance from the
danger zone. Oops! We missed something!

Ah! yes! The moment of impact! But we
can remedy that. Here is an enlargement to
show you exactly what happened.

Mickey Mouse, speechless at his
lucky rescue and absolutely boggled
by the heroic jalopy's action.

Now let's go back to the logical sequence.
BOONG! It isn't easy, steering with a
bull on your bonnet! And you don't have to be

too particular about it, either:
even the best drivers get into
accidents now and again!

Did we say accident? Sorry about
that. Poor old bull: after all he
was minding his own business at first.

But don't let's get all gooey about it.
He seems to have good recuperative powers.
Here he is back on his feet. SNORT!

With the accelerator working overtime,
the jalopy takes advantage of
every ounce of horsepower it has and

takes to its . . . tires! In its headlong drive, it
passes the tree where Mickey, now free
of the red cloak, is helping Minnie down.

"Descend? Are you crazy? I've absolutely
no intention of getting down from here? I want
to climb higher! Give me a push, Mickey!"

"But . . . Minnie! What's gotten into you? Come
down! We've got to get back home!
Quick, let's beat it now while the bull . . .

"THE BULL! As though I didn't know!
I've got to find somewhere
to hide immediately!"

"Do you call that a hiding place? Okay, a
bull's fury is blind, but you're expecting
too much, when you think he won't see you!"

"He saw you, all right! Why not
try talking your way out
of this one? He just might . . . "

"Er . . . Ah . . . Good day, Mr. Bull. Nice
day, isn't it? Lovely weather, makes one
feel real peaceful . . . friendly . . . " SNORT!

—Mickey! If you had to earn your
living by sweet talk, you'd starve!
Fortunately your old jalopy

hasn't forsaken you! Here she is, offering
first-aid, with her radiator
wide open! She surely doesn't plan on . . .

Yes, she does! SNAP! Poor Bull!
Poor tail! After bites like those,
how will he be able to switch away flies!

—Next person that bites me, I swear I'm reporting them to the Society for the Prevention of Cruelty to Animals!

"Don't think about it, bull. . . . See here, I've got something nice for you!"
H'm . . . seems like we're growing real bold!

—Ah! You just know I don't like red. That's mean . . . even for an old, beat-up jalopy!

CLINK CLINK CLINK! Okay, so it's a red light. But how could an honest, angry bull keep from charging it?

CLOPPETTY! CLOPPETTY! CLOPPETTY! Obviously, this one can't. That's why it charges so ferociously.

But the temptress remains perfectly calm, waiting for the right moment, and by a quick switch to the rear wheels, spins them and . . .

SPRIZZ! . . . sends a cloud of mud into the face of the unfortunate bull, who does not seem to appreciate the

beautifying effects of a real mud-pack.
SNORT! BELLOW! GREEEE!
Makes you angry, huh?

Mickey, meanwhile, is arguing with a stubborn Minnie. "Come down! You can't stay up there forever! And don't scream!"

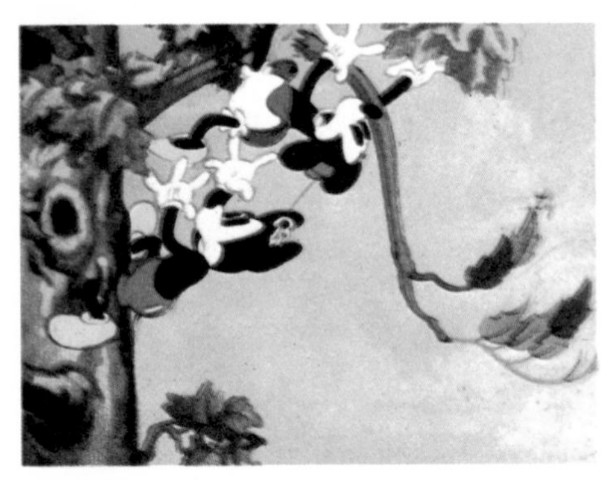

CRACK! But what's the matter with all these cracking boughs? You do more harm than real-estate developers!

"Mickey, Mickey, for the last time DO something!" "What am I supposed to do? Besides falling?" "Mickey, I can NEVER rely on you!"

"Oh! Minnie, this is no time to complain. After all, you're lucky. You've got something soft to fall on!"

"That's all very well . . . but what about you, falling on top of me?" "You're never satisfied!" Look . . . Now you're in the clear. . . .

and it isn't so bad, after all! ROAR! BOOM! Now full gas ahead, before the bull realizes that he needn't go round the tree!

VROOM! VROOM!
CLOPPETTY! CLOP! SNORT!
"He's gaining on us" (CLOPPETTY).

SBUFF! It may not have power steering, but it sure worked. That old jalopy's no dummy.

Poor bull . . . he can't fight modern technology. Well don't you think it's better to call it a day?

BELLOW! Okay by me! But just let those polluters come back again with their smog! They'll see. . . .

"Well, don't look so glum, Mickey! You surely aren't still sulking because of Sharpie?"

"No, Minnie." (But why must we menfolk always be the ones to give in?) "Give me your hand, my love!"

"Friends like we were before, Mickey?" "Like before, Minnie. Like before and like after . . . the film. 'Bye bye, everybody!"

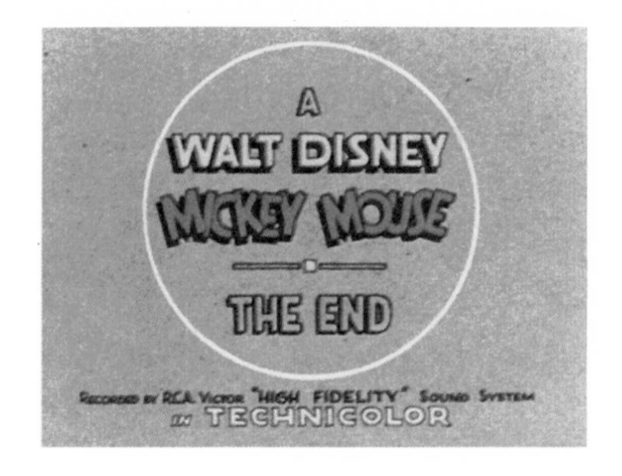

The Brave Little Tailor, 1938

Disney returned to a storybook theme with "Brave Little Tailor," wherein Mickey portrayed the tailor who "slew seven with one blow." Minnie was (naturally) the princess, and the Giant was presumably a close relative to the behemoth in the later feature "Fun and Fancy Free."

That terrible figure on the wall is a giant — a BIG giant.

This poster tells the story. The whole city was frightened.

When they heard the giant was headed their way,

They cleared off the streets and hid in their houses.

Meanwhile, a little tailor named Mickey stitched away

on a coat, even though some pesky flies kept bothering him.

As a matter of fact, lots of flies kept bothering him.

Finally, he put down his needle and grabbed two fly-swatters.

And with one masterful, resounding swat, he hit the attackers.

Not just a teensey swat,
but a decisive SMAASH!

When the dust had lifted, do
you know what he discovered?

He'd killed SEVEN WITH ONE BLOW! "A miracle," he said. "I must tell the town about it."

Well, the townspeople had a giant on
their minds and talked of nothing else.

And so when Tailor Mickey, in
his excitement, stuck his head

out the window and cried
"I just killed seven with one blow!"

What do you think the people
of the town thought?

They thought the little tailor had
killed seven GIANTS with one blow.

The news was so good that the
story spread like wildfire.

Every citizen was excited and
passed the word to his neighbor.

Even babies in their carriages
sat up and took notice.

"Now at last," the townspeople cried,
"the giant has met his match!"

What excitement! What tumult!
What to-ing and fro-ing.

And, as always, the story
grew with the telling.

"SEVEN giants? Oh, come now.
Three or four, maybe, but seven?"

"No, it's true. He killed 'em
. . . and buried 'em too."

Eventually, the word reached
the ears of the king's guards.

One soldier who heard it
was so astounded

that he raced,
clanking in his armor,

straight to the palace and
up the long, stone stairs

to the throne room where
the King held court.

The soldier burst through the door,
pushing servants and courtiers aside,

and, stumbling over his
own feet in his haste,

landed at the King's feet,
somewhat in pieces,

as the screws and bolts of his
armor flew every which way.

The guard caught his breath and,
armorless, whispered to the King.

"By my royal socks!" cried the King.
"He really slew seven?"

"Bring him here at once!" and
the people pushed the tailor forward.

"My tailor? Nonsense. He sews a fine
seam, but . . . YOU slew seven?"

"Yes, Your Majesty. That's true.
Seven with one blow."

"I'm flabbergasted.
Tell me how you did it."

"Well, I was sitting there,
minding my own business . . .

when suddenly these seven big,
ugly, devils appeared out of nowhere

and menaced me. Well, I just
wasn't going to stand for it!"

"Wh-what did you do to them?
(I'm all a-tremble!)"

"I hesitated a moment. Then they
were swarming all over me.

That made me hopping mad!
And I admit I lost my temper.

I saw red and began to beat
them as hard as I could."

"Go on! Go on! You
stood up to all of them?"

"I faced them all and then WHAP!
I let go with a good one.

That did it. I slew all seven.
And about the only thing

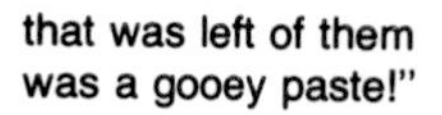

that was left of them
was a gooey paste!"

"Marvelous! I'm exhausted
just listening to your exploits."

"Really, it was nothing. If YOU'D been
there you'd have done the same!"

"This is no time for modesty! As you know, all of us are in gravest danger.

Only you can save us! You must kill the giant who is headed our way."

"S-sire? D-did you s-say — no, you couldn't possibly have . . .

For a second there I thought you told me to go out and kill a giant. . . ."

"I did indeed, my boy. If you can kill seven so easily, what's one more?"

"Er, S-sire, I think there's something you should know first . . . ."

"Oh, I know. You're worried about the reward. Will one chest of gold be sufficient . . . two?"

"Yes, what is it, my dear daughter? . . . I see! I see!"

"All right, dear. Two chests of gold, and the hand of my fair daughter!"

"You're just the bravest man I've ever met!"

SMACK SMACK SMACK.
"Ooooh! I adore you!"

"Boy, if that's part of the reward for killing a giant . . .

Then look out, Giant,
here I come!"

So that's how it happened that the
simple little tailor set forth alone

Across the drawbridge to carry out a mission
from which no-one had ever returned.

"No one's ever r-r-returned?
You mean that?"

"Let me in! Please let me back in!
I'm too young to die!" POUND POUND

"Yoo hoo! Mickey, darling!
Here I am . . . up here."

"Me and my big mouth!
But I don't dare let on to her!"

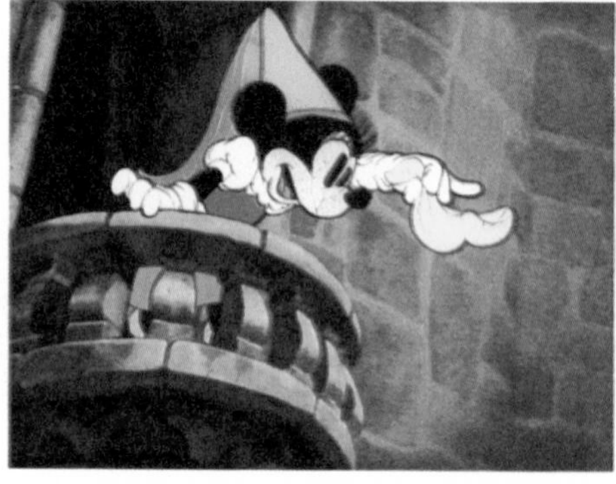

"Go, beloved warrior, and
hasten back to claim my hand."

For a moment, the
tailor's courage returns.

"Now I can't turn back.
I can't let the Princess down!"

But as he reaches the other side
of the drawbridge, fear returns.

"Maybe if I sit here long enough, I'll be
able to think of some way out of this."

"Sure wish it would get dark so I could tiptoe off to a country, where nobody knows me."

"H-hey! I wanted it to get dark fast, but this is ridiculous! Who . . . who . . ."

Who, Mickey? Someone whose shadow looms monstrously over the entire mountain, plain, and town. An evil, shambling shadow!

"H-holy Toledo! It's the G-Giant!"

Mickey races away from a noise like an avalanche as

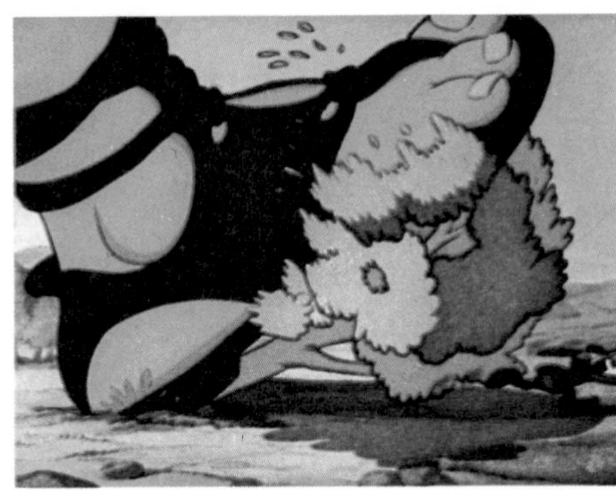

an enormous foot crushes trees in its path.

He races on a little dock and leaps into a rowboat.

The foot is only inches behind him. Mickey rows madly.

The foot hits the water, and the wave it causes

drives the little boat across
the lake like a bullet.

Mickey keeps rowing
right across the beach

up to the yard of a little
straw-covered shed.

The foot looms over him,
and as he dodges,

the shed and its fence are
smashed like match-sticks.

But there's a loaded cart.
"Maybe if I hide in it. . . ."

Just then the Giant decides
to take a little rest.

(Oops! There goes a house!)
And he decides he's hungry.

Pumpkins are his favorite
fruit. Mickey trembles

as the Giant's hand
reaches into the cart.

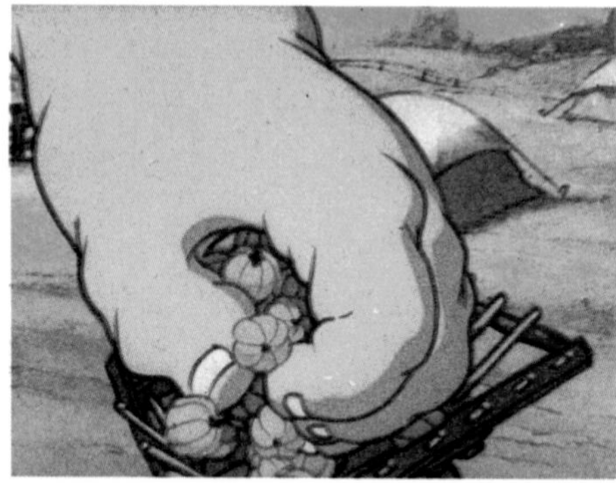

and grabs a handful
of pumpkins—and a mouse!

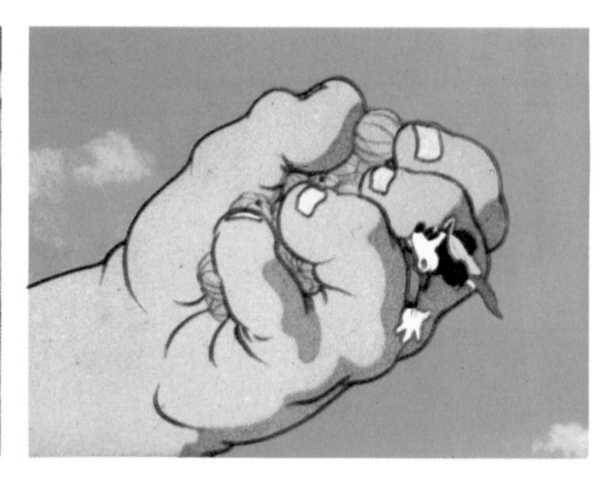

Oh, Mickey! What now?
Can you get out of this fix?

He starts to flip them
into his mouth . . . one, two, three. . . .

But number three is
a desperate Mickey Mouse!

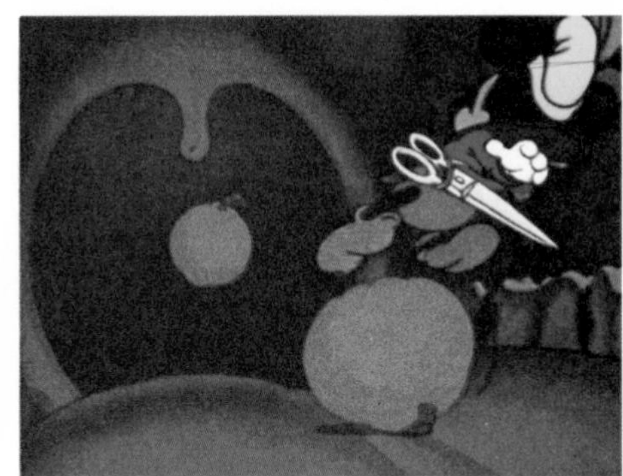

Down, down the Giant's
throat Mickey tumbles,

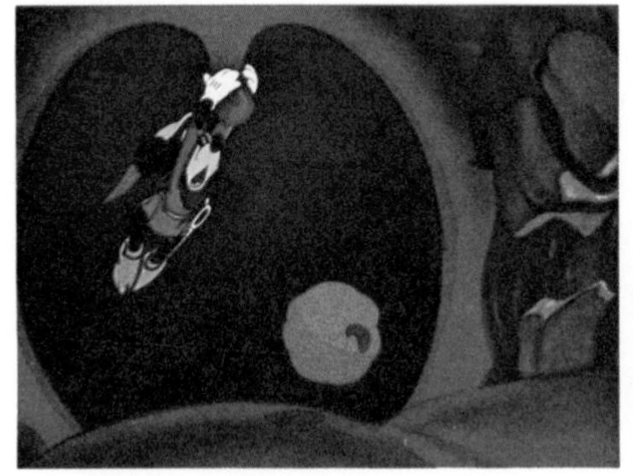

surrounded by pumpkins.
"Oh, so *that's* what tonsils look like!"

And now the Giant
decides he's thirsty.

He sees the well.
That should take care of him.

But remember, please.
This is a pretty stupid fellow.

That silly Giant doesn't just
take a drink — he takes a well.

Meanwhile, Mickey is trying to
escape over a wall of teeth.

Unfortunately, he's a little late.
Here comes the well.

The water hits him like
a monstrous tidal wave.

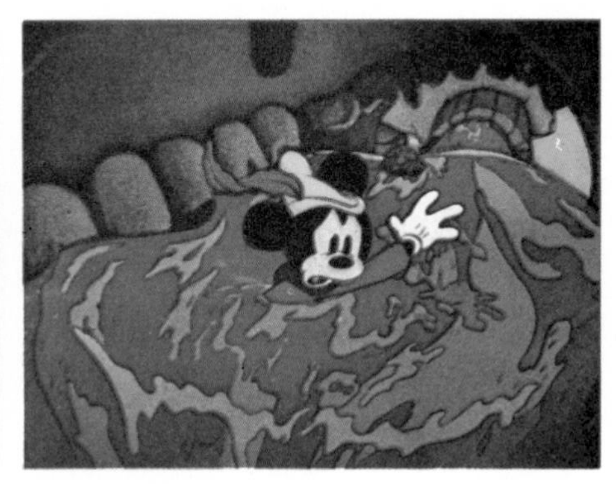

It carries him
back, back, back

and down, down, down into . . .
Oh no! . . . the Giant's stomach!

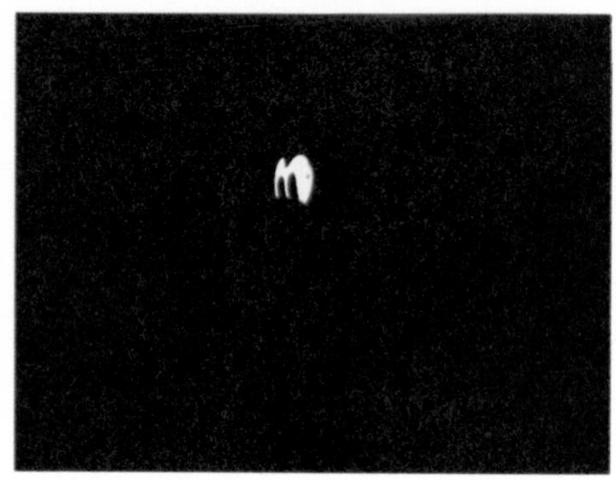

The darkness is as thick
as a feather pillow,

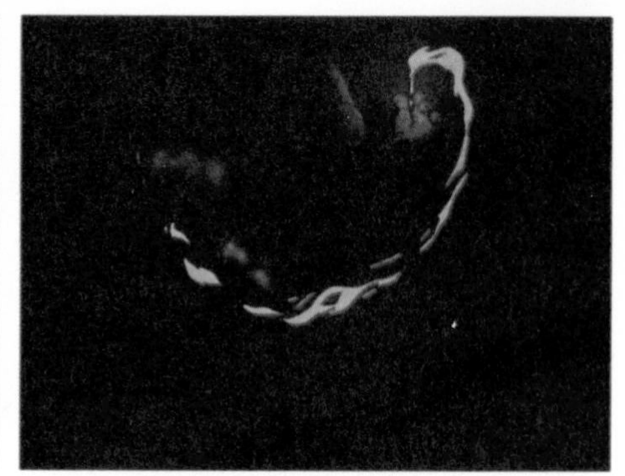

but not so soft. "Well, I'll
strike a match and look around."

He's surrounded by pumpkins . . .
but the bucket saved him . . .

or did it? The Giant gives a
tremendous tug on the well

he still holds in his hand.
Out pops bucket, Mickey, and all.

The little tailor lands
KERPLUNK in a haystack,

which could have been
lucky, except that now

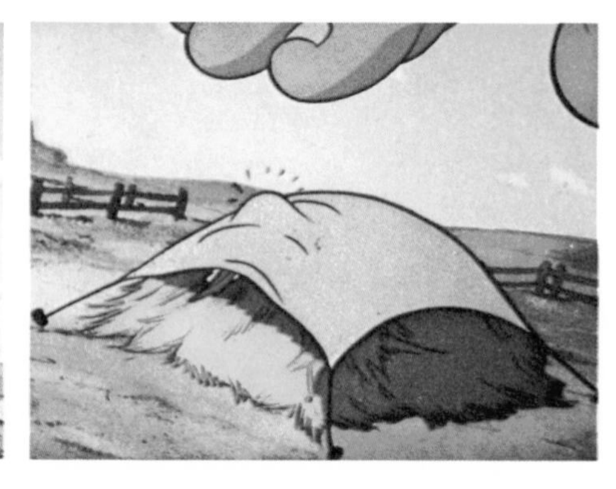

our slow-witted Giant
has still another idea.

He picks up the haystack as if it were a feather
and rolls his own — cigarette that is.

It's an enormous cigarette,
and the Giant is pretty pleased.

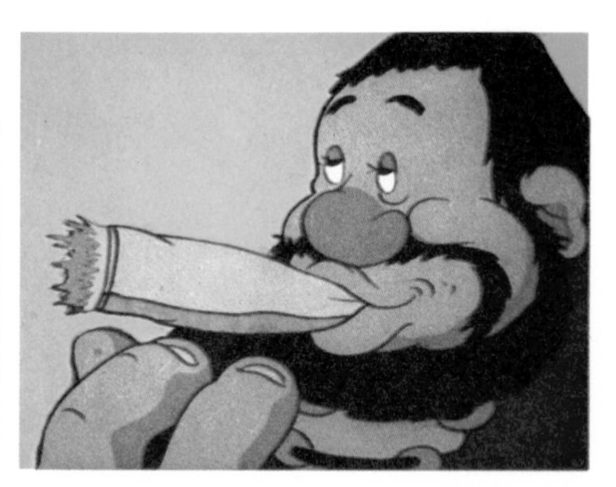

Mickey, of course, is in
there, too. Scarey, isn't it?

"I need a little fire now," decides the big brain.

So he lifts the roof off the house, picks up the stove,

and zip . . . a lighter. "Ah-h-h! First one today."

And the Giant puffs happily . . . for a moment.

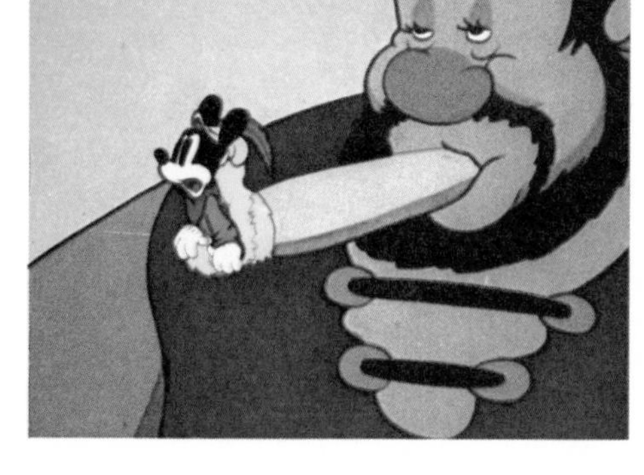

Mickey, desperately, pops out of the end of the "cigarette."

But of course the silly Giant doesn't see him.

His smoke lights up all right, but begins acting strangely.

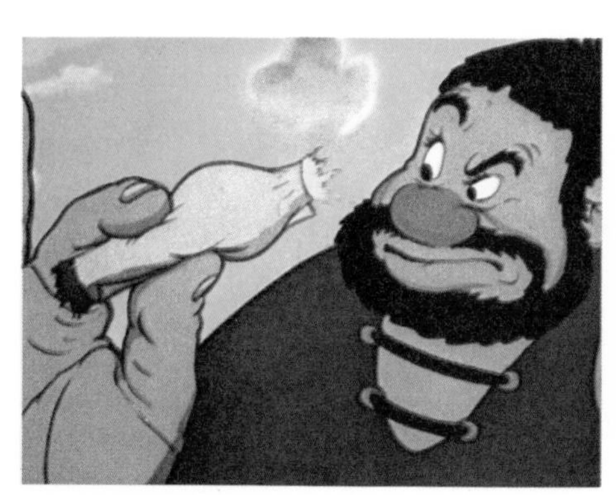

For instance, it pops out in the middle,

then on one end. And as he inspects it more closely,

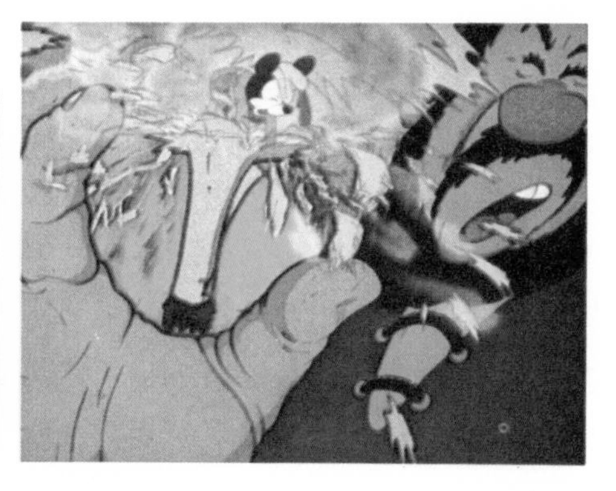

it bursts open like a roman candle on July 4,

burning the giant's lips
and temper to a frazzle.

Because there in his exploding
smoke is a small, scared mouse

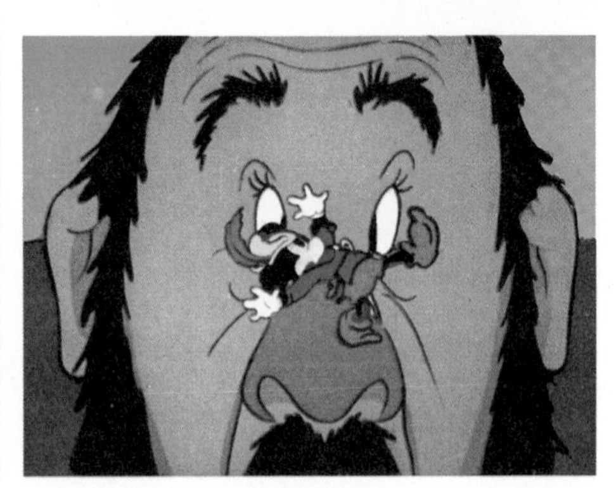

who jumps on the mighty,
broad, red nose,

leaps like an acrobat for
the black, bushy brows,

starts like a mountain climber
up the crinkled forehead,

and OOPS! A flick of that
forehead sends the mouse

hurtling back into the palm
of that huge, horrid hand.

"You insect! You less-than-worm!
You . . . you NOTHING!

Here's what happens
to pests like you!"

Mickey might be small
but he's fast . . . very fast.

"Where'd he go? Where'd he go?
I coulda sworn . . ."

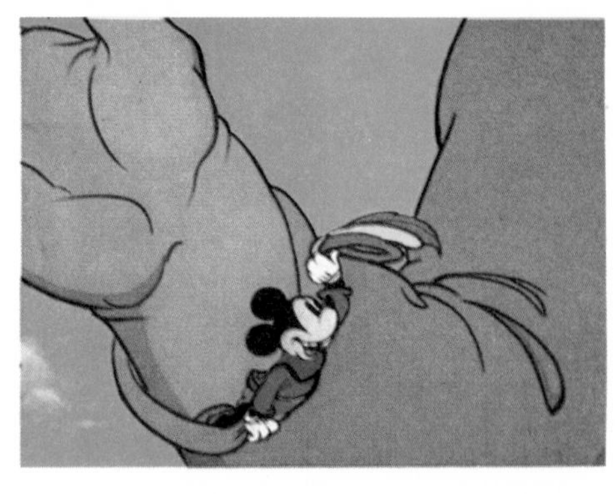

"Yoo-hoo! Here I am, you
big, dumb, stupid, FAT moron."

"So I'm FAT am I?
I'll get you for that!"

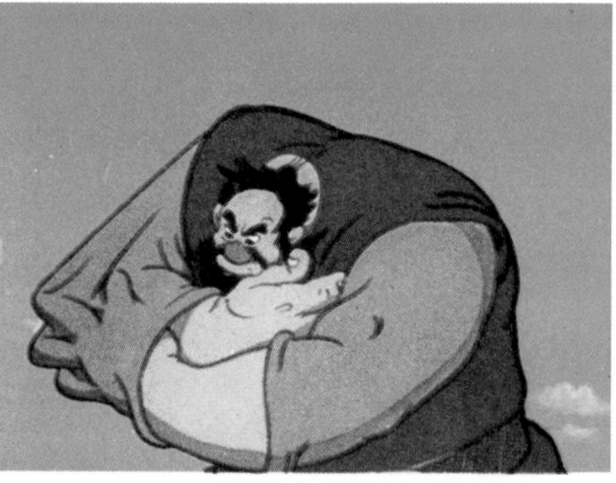

But the little tailor has
raced up the Giant's sleeve

and is cutting an escape hatch
up near the shoulder.

(He's been a tailor too long
to travel without his tools.)

Uh-oh. The mammoth fist
has popped through the hole.

Mickey is ready. Armed now
with his needle and thread,

he quickly stitches the
hand in place. Like a flash

he lassoes the pudgy
nose, yanks it back

and ties it to a wiry lock
of long, greasy hair.

Now, with a leap, he
starts the rest of his journey.

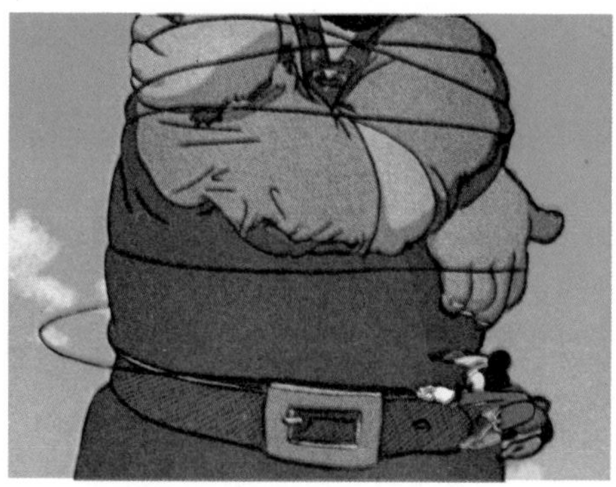

Round and round the Giant's
enormous body he goes,

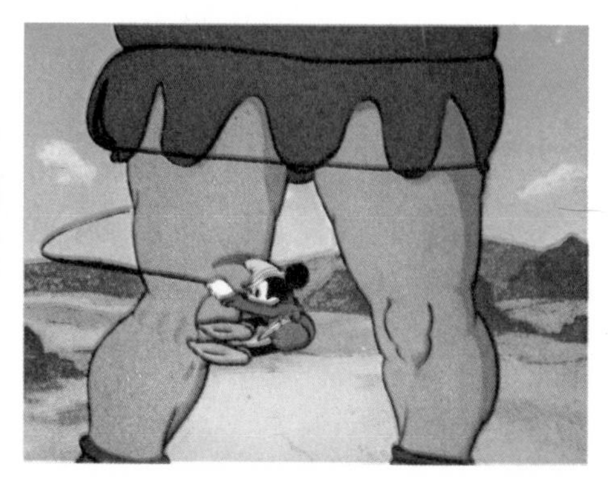

binding the monster as
tight as ever he can.

Now only a single jerk on
the strong black thread

sends the teetering titan
smashing to the ground,

Where he lies — well, you
might say, a sleeping Giant.

And you know, our story has a
happy ending, even for the Giant.

All he has to do is lie
there and breathe heavily.

His breath runs a windmill that
powers an amusement park

with a merry-go-round
that was a great favorite

of the King, who always fell
off a real, live horse,

and of Mickey and the
Princess, too. But maybe

they liked it for entirely
different reasons . . .

which seems to please the
King very much, indeed.

and that's as good a way
to end this story as any.

Mickey and the Pirates, 1934

The *Mickey and the Pirates* story ran on newspaper comics pages from January 7 to April 17, 1934, and was syndicated by King Features. An average of 5 million Americans read it daily. Drawn by Floyd Gottfredson and written by Merrill de Maris, this superb story shows Mickey at his apex.

TAKING A LOAD OF FOOD TO THE SNOWBOUND CITIZENS OF ROCK LEDGE, MICKEY AND MINNIE SEE A STORM APPROACHING

DISASTER THREATENS! HEADED FOR ROCK LEDGE MICKEY'S PLANE IS WEIGHED DOWN WITH SNOW ON THE WINGS AND ---

FLYING A CARGO OF FOOD TO SNOWBOUND ROCK LEDGE, MICKEY AND MINNIE BARELY ESCAPE DISASTER!

LOSING THEIR PROPELLER, HIGH IN THE MOUNTAINS, MICKEY AND MINNIE ARE DIVING TOWARD DESTRUCTION!

M-M-MICKEY! ARE WE REALLY FALLING?

I'LL SAY WE ARE! GET READY TO BAIL OUT!

ALMOST IN SIGHT OF ROCK LEDGE, MICKEY'S GAS TANK IS PUNCTURED BY SHOTS FROM AN UNKNOWN ENEMY! AND IT IS NEARLY EMPTY!

THE FOOD HAS BEEN DELIVERED TO SNOWBOUND ROCK LEDGE-- BUT MICKEY'S PLANE IS OUT OF GAS

THE FOOD IS DELIVERED! BUT MICKEY AND MINNIE ARE STRANDED IN A BIG PINE TREE, HIGH ABOVE SNOWBOUND "ROCK LEDGE"!

?
© 1934, by Walt Disney Enterprises, Great Britain rights reserved

WE'D LIKE TO GO TO THE HOTEL, PLEASE! AND DIDN'T YOUR MOTHER EVER TELL YOU IT ISN'T POLITE TO STARE AT PEOPLE?
?
WALT DISNEY

YE SURE SAVED US FROM STARVIN' WHEN YE BRUNG IN THAT FOOD! NOW MEBBE WE'LL BE ABLE T'GIT ALONG TILL SPRING!
SPRING! WILL YA HAFTA WAIT THAT LONG FOR MORE FOOD?

SURE! THAR'S THIRTY FEET O' SNOW ON THE TRAIL! NOBODY CAN'T GIT IN OR OUT O'HERE — - NOT EVEN ON SNOW-SHOES!
!

YA SEE, THAR AIN'T NO ROADS UP HERE EVEN IN SUMMER! WE PACK ALL OUR SUPPLIES IN ON MULES! AN THE NEAREST TOWN'S A HUNDRED MILES AWAY!
GOODNESS! HOW TERRIBLE!

I WOULDN'T THINK OF STAYING IN SUCH A PLACE! WHEN DOES THE NEXT TRAIN LEAVE?
!
!
WALT DISNEY

ALL TH' FOLKS IN "ROCK LEDGE" THINK YER HEROES, BRINGIN' US FOOD THE WAY YA DID!
THESE PEOPLE DO, MEBBE, BUT SOMEBODY DOESN'T!
© 1934 by Walt Disney Enterprises. Great Britain rights reserved

A COUPLE O' SHOTS WAS FIRED AT US WHILE WE WAS FLYIN' OVER THAT GRAVEL PILE JUST OUT O' TOWN!

GOSH WHACKY, SON! THAT AIN'T GRAVEL! IT'S A GOLD MINE! BUT IT'S CLOSED DOWN FOR THE WINTER! THERE AIN'T NOBODY UP THERE!
?
!

SO, YA SEE, THERE COULDN'T O' BEEN NO SHOTS! IT'S IMPOSSIBLE!
WELL, I WISH YA'D CLIMB UP AN' WHISPER THAT TO OUR GAS TANK! IT'S GOT TWO BULLET HOLES IN IT!
1-31
WALT DISNEY

I TELL YA THERE WAS SOMEBODY UP AT TH' GOLD MINE! AN I'VE GOT TWO BULLET HOLES IN MY PLANE TO PROVE IT!
WELL-- MEBBE! BUT I AIN'T GONNA CLIMB UP T' FIND OUT!
© 1934 by Walt Disney Enterprises. Great Britain rights reserved

BUT AIN'T YA GONNA DO SOME-- THING ABOUT IT? IT'S DANGEROUS, HAVIN' GUYS LIKE THAT AROUND!
I SHOULD SAY SO! WHY, PEOPLE HAVE BEEN KILLED BY BEING SHOT AT!
2-1

ALL RIGHT! HAVE IT YER OWN WAY! TH' MINE'S FULL O' SOLJERS, AN' BANDITS, AN' CANNIBALS, AN' MACHINE GUNS, AN' CANNONS AN' BATTLESHIPS!
OH, MY GOODNESS! IS IT REALLY?

NO, IT AIN'T! THERE'S NOBODY UP THAR AN' THAT ENDS IT!
AN' ANYWAY TH' SHERIFF DON'T WANT T' BOTHER 'EM!

MICKEY, WE JUST CAN'T STAY IN "ROCK LEDGE" UNTIL SPRING! ISN'T THERE SOME WAY TO GET OUT?
I DUNNO! I'VE BEEN THINKIN'! AN' MEBBE I'VE GOT AN IDEA!

YOU KNOW HOW TH' NAVY LAUNCHES PLANES OFF BATTLESHIPS! THEY START TH' MOTOR, AN' THEN SHOOT 'EM OFF WITH A CATAPULT!

WELL, IF WE COULD GET A LOT OF MEN AND PULL THAT TREE DOWN AN' THEN LET IT FLY BACK-- IT'D BE TH' SAME AS A CATAPULT -- AN' AWAY WE'D GO!

LISSEN, SON! IF YA WANTA COMMIT SUICIDE USE THIS! IT'D SAVE EVERYBODY A LOT O' TROUBLE!
2-2
WALT DISNEY

WITH BLOCK AND TACKLE AND A LARGE CREW OF MEN, THE HUGE PINE TREE, HOLDING THE PLANE, IS BENT DOWN TO THE GROUND,

READY TO CATAPULT MICKEY AND MINNIE INTO THE AIR!

WITH A GIANT PINE TREE FOR A CATAPULT, MICKEY AND MINNIE ARE READY TO LEAVE ROCK LEDGE!

A MIGHTY **SWISH**, AND THE PLANE IS SHOT INTO THE AIR! BUT---

25

SKIRTING ALONG THE GROUND, MICKEY IS TRYING TO GET HIS PLANE UNDER CONTROL!

HIS PLANE OUT OF CONTROL, MICKEY SWOOPS DOWN OVER THE GOLD MINE THROUGH A BARRAGE OF BULLETS AND ACCIDENTALLY PICKS UP TWO SACKS OF GOLD!

BWOOOM!
CRACK!

MINNIE! THIS ISN'T FOG AT ALL — IT'S CLOUDS! WE'RE GETTIN' INTO ANOTHER STORM!
WELL - WHAT DO YOU WANT ME TO DO ABOUT IT ? BLOW IT AWAY ?
WALT DISNEY

WE'VE GOTTA STAY ABOVE THAT STORM! IT'S RAININ' SOUP AN' FISH DOWN BELOW!
YES, BUT IT'S AWFUL COLD UP THIS HIGH! I'M -- I'M FREEZING!

CRAACKLE!
CRASH!
BOOM!
EEEEEK!

GOOD GOSH! THAT WAS CLOSE! ARE YA ALL RIGHT, MINNIE ?
YES! I'M MUCH BETTER, THANKS!

I HAVEN'T BEEN SO WARM SINCE WE LEFT HOME!
WALT DISNEY

FLYING ABOVE A TERRIFIC STORM, MICKEY'S PLANE IS STRUCK BY LIGHTNING!

2-14

POOR MICKEY AND MINNIE- FLYING IN A STORM NEARLY OUT OF GAS AND WITH THE RUDDER BURNED OFF!

GOSH! IF I COULD ONLY FIGURE OUT SOME WAY T' GET DOWN!
OH, MICKEY! I JUST THOUGHT OF SOMETHING!
© 1934, by Walt Disney Enterprises, Great Britain rights reserved
2-15

YA DID? WHAT?
I FORGOT TO TELL OUR DAIRYMAN TO STOP DELIVERING MILK!

OH, BOY! WHAT A WIND! I GOT NO MORE IDEA WHERE WE'RE GOIN' THAN A RABBIT!
© 1934, by Walt Disney Enterprises, Great Britain rights reserved

IT'S LUCKY ONLY THE RUDDER WAS BURNED OFF AN' NOT THE ELEVATORS OR WE'D O' BEEN DEAD LONG AGO!

ARE WE OFF OUR COURSE, MICKEY?
COURSE! SAY, WITH OUR RUDDER GONE WE'VE GOT NO COURSE!

WE JUST GO WHERE TH' WIND TAKES US!
WALT DISNEY
2-16

AS NIGHT FALLS, MICKEY'S RUDDERLESS PLANE FLIES OUT OF THE RAINSTORM INTO A BLINDING FOG!

2.17

SPUT - SPUT - SPUTTER FFFFFTT'

GOOD GOSH! WE'RE OUT O' GAS! IT'S ALL OVER, NOW!

PITCH BLACK NIGHT! HEAVY FOG! UNKNOWN TERRITORY! AND MICKEY HAS TO MAKE A DEAD-STICK LANDING IN A RUDDERLESS PLANE! WHAT A PREDICAMENT!

IN THE DEAD OF NIGHT, MICKEY'S DISABLED PLANE -- BLOWN FAR OFF ITS COURSE- CRASHES INTO A LINE OF TELEGRAPH WIRES!

!
HEY YOU! WOT ARE YA DOIN' UP THERE?

COME DOWN OFFA THAT OR I'LL PLUG YA!

SWEET BILGEWATER! A DAME! HAW! THE CAPTAIN'LL LIKE THAT!

AHOY, CAP'N! LEMME SHOW YA A COUPLE O' BOIDIES I FOUND PERCHIN' ON THE AERIAL!
CAPTAIN
?

WELL, BLAST ME EYELIDS! LOOK WHO'S HERE!
PEG-LEG PETE!!
WALT DISNEY — 2 21

SO YA WAS TRYIN' TO SPY ON ME AGAIN, HUH?
SPY NUTHIN', YOU BIG GORILLA! WE LANDED ON YOUR OLD SHIP BY ACCIDENT!

ALL WE WANT FROM YOU, PETE, IS PASSAGE BACK TO LAND! WE'LL PAY YOU FOR IT, WITH OUR TWO BAGS OF GOLD!
HAW! HAW! HAW! BEFORE YOU GIT OFF THIS SHIP YOU'LL PAY FOR A LOT O' THINGS!
ROCK LEDGE MINING CO.
ROCK LEDGE MINING CO.
© 1934, by Walt Disney Enterprises, Great Britain rights reserved

AN' IF YA WASN'T SPYIN' ON ME, WHAT'RE YA DOIN' WITH THIS GOLD FROM ROCK LEDGE, HEY ?
FROM - - ? WELL, FER - - - SAY! WHAT DO YOU KNOW ABOUT THAT MINE ?
$ ROCK LEDGE MINING CO.
ROCK LEDGE $

ME ? HAW! HAW! HAW! I KNOW PLENTY!

I'VE SWIPED ENOUGH GOLD OUTA ROCK LEDGE MINE T' MAKE ME RICH! SEE? AN' JUST T' SHOW YA WHO'S CAPTAIN ON THIS BOAT - - -

SOCK!

AN' NOW THAT WE'VE GOT THAT LITTLE SISSY OUT O' TH' WAY, LET'S ME AN' YOU GET FRIENDLY!
WHY, YOU - - - YOU - - !!

ATTA GIRL! I LIKES 'EM WITH SPIRIT! HOW'S ABOUT GIVIN' POPPA A NICE BIG KISS ? HUH ?

NO KISS FOR POPPA, HUH?
YOU LET ME GO, OR I'LL SLAP YOUR FACE-- GOOD!
!

O.K., BEBBY! SLAP IT!
!

!

BONK!

?
?!
WELL, I'LL BE A BOILED LOBSTER!
WALT DISNEY

PETE, WAS THAT YOUR MEN SHOOTIN' AT US IN ROCK LEDGE?
SURE' THEY'VE BEEN SWIPIN' GOLD UP THERE ALL WINTER! I TOLD 'EM TO SHOOT ANYBODY WHO CAME NEAR TH' MINE!
!

I SHIPPED ALL TH' GOLD DOWN HERE TO THE BOAT BY PLANE! TH' LAST LOAD WAS READY T' BE PICKED UP WHEN YOU FLEW BY AN' NABBED IT BY ACCIDENT!
!

YA SEE, BEBBY, I'VE DECIDED T' GO STRAIGHT! AN' THE ONLY WAY T' SET MYSELF UP IN AN HONEST BUSINESS WAS T' SWIPE THE MONEY!
BUT--- BUT WHAT BUSINESS ARE YOU IN?

SMUGGLING!
2-26
WALT DISNEY

HODDA DO, DEAR SIR AND (WOOP! PARDON!) MADAM? MY NAME'S HICKUP!
HOWDA DO?
© 1934, by Walt Disney Enterprises, Great Britain rights reserved

I AM PEGLEG PETE'S BODYGUARD, ASSISTANT, ADVISER, JESTER, COUNSELLOR AND PUNCHING-BAG!
WHAT'S PETE GONNA DO WITH US? WHERE'S OUR BAGS O' GOLD?

HE WILL PUT YOU ASHORE AS SOON AS WE LAND! THE GOLD HE WILL KEEP AS PAYMENT FOR YOUR (WOOP! PARDON!) PASSAGE!

WE'RE IN A HURRY T' GET HOME, WHAT PORT ARE WE HEADIN' FOR, AN' HOW FAR AWAY IS IT?
2-27

TAKOOLI ISLAND, IN THE SOUTH SEAS! ABOUT 5000 MILES FROM HERE!
WALT DISNEY

SAY, HICKUP! IS IT ALL RIGHT FOR MINNIE AN' ME T' GO OUT ON DECK?
OH, YEAH! SURE! I FORGOT! THAT'S WHAT I CAME IN TO (WOOP! PARDON!) TELL YOU!

PLEASE, MR HICKUP! DO YOU KNOW WHAT PEG LEG PETE IS PLANNING TO DO WITH US?
YES, HE'S GOING TO MARRY YOU AS SOON AS HE GETS AROUND TO IT!
NICE WEATHER WE'RE HAVING, ISN'T IT?

AS FOR MICKEY, PETE'S OFFERED A PRIZE TO THE MAN WHO SUGGESTS THE MOST ARTISTIC AND HORRIBLE DEATH!
NICE SHIP THIS, DON'T YOU THINK?

THE LAST TIME WE CAME ALONG HERE, THERE WAS A SCHOOL OF PORPOISES!
MY, MY, MY! I HOPE THEY'RE STILL HERE!
WALT DISNEY 2-28

MINNIE, WE'RE SURE IN A TOUGH SPOT! WE GOTTA DO SOME SERIOUS THINKIN'! PEG LEG PETE MEANS BUSINESS!
?

HE HATES ME AN' WANTS T' KILL ME! HE LOVES YOU AN' WANTS T' MARRY YA! WE GOTTA DO SOMETHIN' AN' DO IT QUICK!

WE'RE IN DANGER EVERY MINUTE WE'RE ON BOARD! SHALL WE TRY TO ESCAPE IN A LIFEBOAT OR SHALL WE START FIGHTIN' ?

WHAT DO YOU THINK ABOUT IT ?
PARDON ME, MICKEY! I DIDN'T HEAR A WORD YOU SAID!
3-1

DON'T YOU THINK MY NEW HAT IS CUTE ?
WALT DISNEY

HULLO, SWEETIE! HOW'S ABOUT A KISS FOR POPPA ?
YOU LEAVE HER ALONE, YOU BIG GORILLA!
© 1934 by Walt Disney Enterprises Great Britain rights reserved

DON'T BOTHER ME! I'M BUSY!
YA SEE, I BEEN LONESOME! I FIGGER WHAT THIS SHIP NEEDS IS THUH DAINTY TOUCH OF A WOMAN'S HAND!

WELL, HERE'S A TOUCH ---- AND HERE'S ANOTHER!
SMACK!
3-2

HAW! HAW! HAW! THAT'S THUH SPIRIT! SLAP MY FACE --- I LIKES IT!!

BUT DON'T YUH TRY IT AGAIN --- SEE ?

LISSEN, PEGLEG PETE! DO WHAT YOU WANT WITH ME, BUT YOU LEAVE MINNIE ALONE! UNDERSTAND?
PIPE DOWN, YA RAT! OR I'LL RAM MY FIST CLEAN DOWN YER THROAT!
!

YOU'VE TRIED T' KILL ME A DOZEN TIMES, BUT I'M STILL HERE, AIN'T I? I CAN LICK YOU AN' YER WHOLE CREW PUT TOGETHER!
OF COURSE, HE CAN! DON'T YOU EVER READ THE COMIC STRIPS?
by Walt Disney Enterprises Great Britain rights reserved

GOSH! MEBBE THEY'RE RIGHT! MEBBE CRIME DON'T PAY! MEBBE I CAN'T WIN!

THAT SETTLES IT! I'M GONNA REFORM! I HAVE REFORMED! I'M A GOOD GUY FROM NOW ON!

OH·H·H·H! TO THINK O' TH' WICKED LIFE I'VE LED!
?
?
3-5
WALT DISNEY

IT AIN'T NO EASY JOB FER A GUY AS TOUGH AS ME TUH REFORM! BUT I DECIDED TO DO IT! I'LL BE AS PURE AS A LILY!
THAT'S FINE, MR. PETE! IT-IT MAKES ME FEEL MUCH SAFER!

HAW! HAW! HAW! SURE YOU'LL BE SAFE! WE'RE GONNA GIT MARRIED, AN' I'LL PROTECT YUH!
!

YUH SEE, MINNIE, WHEN A GUY LIKE I IS REFORMIN', WHAT HE NEEDS IS THUH TENDER LOVE OF A BEE-YOOTIFUL WOMAN!

WHAT'S MORE, I'M GONNA GIT YUH, IF I HAVE T' BREAK THE NECK OF EVERY BLANKETTY- -BLANK SWAB ON DIS SHIP!

DON'T FORGIT, GAL! WE'RE GONNA GIT MARRIED, SO'S YUH CAN REFORM ME!

C'MON! GIVE POPPA A KISS!
YUH'LL GIT USED TUH ME ONCE WE'RE HITCHED!

TAKE THAT, YOU BIG GORILLA! AN' THAT! AN' THAT!
HEY! LEGGO MY-- ! HEY! CUT IT OUT! TAKE 'IM OFF! HEY!

ALL HANDS ON DECK! ALL HANDS ON DECK! MUTINY! MUTINY!

HELP! HELP! MUTINY! TAKE 'IM OFF!

HE WAS MAKIN' LOVE TO MINNIE! LEMME GO! I'LL TEAR HIM APART!

SOCK THUH CAPTAIN, WILL YUH? THAT'S MUTINY!

TAKE 'IM AWAY! AN STRING HIM UP ON A YARDARM! I'LL SHOW YUH HOW WE TREAT MUTINEERS ON THIS SHIP!

YOU CAN'T GET AWAY WITH IT, PEGLEG PETE! I'LL GET YOU--AN' YOUR WHOLE SMUGGLING GANG WITH YOU!
YEAH? EVEN AFTER I HANGS YUH TO A YARDARM, EH? HAW! HAW! HAW!

AVAST, YUH SWABS! UP WITH THE MUTINEER! HOIST AWAY!

OW-OOO!!
HOIST AWAY NUTHIN!

HEY! STOP HIM! PULL HIM DOWN!
I CAN'T- THERE'S A KNOT IN THE ROPE!

LISSEN, YA BIG, DUMB OX! NEXT TIME YA TRY T' HANG A GUY, MAKE SURE YA GOT HIS HANDS TIED!
3 9

UP AFTER HIM, YA SWABS! BRING 'IM DOWN, DEAD OR ALIVE!
!

YAAAAHH! COME ON UP! I DARE YA TO! I DARE YA TO!

WELL-- I WARNED YA!
?
!

3/10

COME ON DOWN, YA RAT! I'M WAITIN' FOR YUH!

HEY, GANG! COME ON! I'VE GOT HIM! I'VE GOT 'IM!
© 1934, by Walt Disney Enterprises, Great Britain rights reserved 8-12

WALT DISNEY

AFTER HIM, MEN! GIT 'IM --- DEAD OR ALIVE!
Walt Disney Enterprises, Great Britain rights reserved

COME BACK, YA RAT --- AN' FIGHT!

O. K. ---
HAVE IT YER OWN WAY!
3·13

I WARNED YA, PETE! BEFORE I GET THROUGH WITH YOU AN' YER SMUGGLING CREW, YOU'LL WISH YOU HAD REFORMED!

YEAH? WELL, HOW DO YUH LIKE THESE ONIONS?

YUH LITTLE RAT!

YEE-OWW!!

WHERE'S THAT BLANKETTY-BLANK (PUFF! PUFF!) CREW GONE? I'M GETTIN' TOO FAT FER DIS KIND O' WORK!

HEY! YA DISH-FACED SWABS! HELP ME CAPTURE THIS ※*☆*☆ MUTINEER! WHERE'S HE GONE --- THUH RAT?

HE'S NOWHERE IN SIGHT! I'LL JUST HIDE IN THIS BARREL UNTIL IT GETS DARK!

WALT DISNEY 3-15

AVAST, YA SWABS! STRING 'IM UP! AN' DON'T FERGIT TUH TIE HIS HANDS, NEITHER!!

LAND AHOY! LAND AHOY!
WOT'S DAT?

SORRY TO INTERRUPT YOUR (WOOP! PARDON!) FUN, BUT WE'VE JUST SIGHTED TAKOOLI ISLAND!
WELL, BLAST ME EYELIDS!

PUT 'IM IN IRONS AN' THROW HIM IN THUH HOLD! WE'LL TEND TUH HIM ON TH' WAY BACK HOME!
!
3-16
WALT DISNEY

YOU GUARD HIM WHILE I'M ASHORE, HICKUP!
AN' DO YUH KNOW WOT I'LL DO TO YUH IF THAT RAT GITS LOOSE?
NO, SIR!
!

BOP!! BOP!! BOP!

THAT'S WOT I'D DO! SEE?
!

DO YOU KNOW, MICKEY— I REALLY BELIEVE HE WOULD, TOO!
?
?
3-17
WALT DISNEY

PEGLEG PETE'S SMUGGLING SHIP HAS LANDED AT **TAKOOLI ISLAND**, TO TAKE ON A CONTRABAND CARGO!

GIT READY! CAST OFF!
WHAT DOES HE MEAN, "CAST OFF"? IS HE KNITTING SOMETHING?
!
Walt Disney Enterprises, Great Britain rights reserved

KNITTING, MY EYE! IT MEANS TH' SHIP'S LOADED, AN' WE'RE STARTIN' HOME WITH THIS CARGO OF OPIUM! WE'RE IN A TOUGH SPOT!
3-21

HEY, HICKUP! HOW LONG DO I HAFTA STAY CHAINED UP LIKE THIS?
ONLY ABOUT AN HOUR LONGER!
THAT'S GOOD!
YEAH--

THEN PETE'S GONNA TAKE YA OUT AN' (WOOP! PARDON!) HANG YA TO A YARDARM!
!
WALT DISNEY

DON'T KID ME, HICKUP! PEGLEG PETE WOULDN'T TRUST YOU WITH TH' KEYS TO THESE PADLOCKS!
SURE, HE WOULD! I'VE GOT 'EM RIGHT IN MY POCKET!

BETCHA A DOLLAR!
TEN DOLLARS!
A HUNDRED DOLLARS!
A THOUSAND!
A MILLION!
A BILLION!
TWO BITS!
CASH?
SURE!

PEGLEG PETE'S SMUGGLING SHIP IS LOADED WITH OPIUM, AND HEADED FOR HOME WITH ITS CONTRABAND CARGO!

WHADDAYA MEAN, YUH WANTA BE FRIENDS?
PETE, WE'VE BEEN SCRAPPIN' FOR A LONG TIME, AN' WHERE ARE WE? I'M STILL ALIVE AN' YOU'RE STILL RUNNIN' AROUND LOOSE!
© 1934 by Walt Disney Enterprises. Great Britain rights reserved

SO LET'S QUIT BUCKIN' EACH OTHER, AN' GET TOGETHER!
YUH MEAN YUH WANT ME T' GO STRAIGHT?
NO! I MEAN I WANT T' GO CROOKED!

MICKEY MOUSE! HAVE YOU LOST YOUR MIND?
NAW! I'M JUST GETTIN' SOME SENSE AT LAST! FROM NOW ON, PETE AN' I ARE GONNA BE PALS IN CRIME!
?

OOH!
AIN'T WE, PETE?
WHADDAYA MEAN 'AIN'T WE'? I DON'T GIT IT— WOT'S D' GAG?
WALT DISNEY
3-26

WHAT'S YER GAME, YA RAT?
GOSH, PETE, I'M NOT PLAYIN' A GAME! I'M SERIOUS! I WANTA BE YOUR FRIEND!
© 1934, by Walt Disney Enterprises. Great Britain rights reserved

I LIKE BRAINS--- AN' YOU'VE GOT 'EM! THAT'S WHY YOU'RE STILL FREE! YOU'RE TOO SMART FOR THE COPS!
SURE, I AM! WHY, I'VE GOT BRAINS I AIN'T EVEN USED YET!

WHAT I ADMIRE ABOUT YOU IS, YOU'RE SUCH A BIG MAN IN YOUR BUSINESS! YOU'RE PROBABLY TH' WORST CROOK THAT EVER LIVED!
AWWW--I BET YOU TELL DAT TO EVERYBODY!

YOU'RE A SMUGGLER, A KIDNAPER, A BANK-ROBBER AN' A MURDERER! HOW'D YA EVER GET SO--SO--SMART?
GAWSH I DUNNO MICKEY! I GUESS IT JEST COMES NATCHERAL--- SAME AS ME GOOD LOOKS!
?
?
3-27
WALT DISNEY

BUT, MICKEY! IF YOU'RE GOING TO BE PALS WITH PETE, WHAT'S GOING TO HAPPEN TO ME?
DON'T WORRY ABOUT THAT! PETE'S A SWELL GUY! WHY DON'T YA MARRY HIM?
!

WHY, MICKEY MOUSE! I'D RATHER DIE! WHY, YOU--- YOU--YOU-
BUT, MINNIE- I---- I----- YA SEE----

YES, I SEE EVERYTHING! YOU TRAITOR! YOU COWARD! TAKE THAT!
?
SMACK!

OH! BOO HOO HOO!
AW--GEE, MINNIE! YA SHOULDN'T O' DONE THAT! I'M DOIN' IT FER YER OWN GOOD! HONEST I AM! HONEST, MINNIE! CAN'T YA- -CAN'T YA TRUST ME?
HAW! HAW! HAW!
3-28
WALT DISNEY

PETE CAUGHT MICKEY SLIPPING MINNIE A NOTE, READING:

"I'VE GOT A PLAN. DO WHAT I SAY, AND DON'T ARGUE. PLAY UP TO PEGLEG PETE. DON'T WORRY. TRUST ME."

IT SAYS --- IT SAYS --- "DEAR MINNIE: CAPTAIN PETE'S A SWELL GUY! I KNOW YOU'D LIKE HIM IF --- IF YOU KNEW HIM BETTER — YOURS TRULY — MICKEY MOUSE" — THAT'S WHAT IT SAYS!

THAT'S GOOD! THASS SWELL! I KNEW YUH WAS MY PAL, MICKEY!
THAT LETTER SETTLES IT!
GOOD GOIN', MINNIE! I --- I COULD KISS YA FOR THAT!
3-30
WALT DISNEY

MICKEY, IF YA FIX IT SO'S ME AN' MINNIE KIN GIT MARRIED, I'LL MAKE YUH ME PARTNER, AN' GIVE YUH HALF O' DIS BOAT!
DON'T WORRY, PETE, OL' PAL, OL' PAL! I'LL FIX IT FOR YA!

LISSEN, MINNIE! PLAY UP TO PETE! MAKE HIM THINK YA LIKE HIM! YA GOTTA DO IT! IT'S OUR ONLY CHANCE! SEE?
NO, I DON'T! BUT -- I'LL DO IT!
ATTA GIRL!

IT'S O.K., PETE! SHE SAYS SHE'S ALL FOR YA!
I KNEW IT! I KNEW SHE COULDN'T RESIST ME!
3-31

WHOOPEE! SHE LOVES ME! I'M THUH HAPPIEST
SWAB IN THUH WORLD! WHOOPEE!
?
?
CAPTAIN'S CABIN

Y-Y-YES! BUT I'D RATHER D-D-DIE! BOO-HOO-HOOOO!

WHOOPEE! SHE LOVES ME! SHE LOVES ME! I KNEW SHE COULDN'T RESIST A HANDSOME SWAB LIKE ME!
WALT DISNEY

HEY, FELLERS! HAVE YA HEARD TH' NEWS? MINNIE'S GONNA MARRY CAPTAIN PETE!
YEAH, YUH YELLOW RAT! WE HEARD!

YOU AIN'T KIDDIN' US-- SAVIN' YER OWN NECK BY MAKIN' YER GIRL MARRY A BELLOWIN' DOG LIKE PETE! IT'S ENOUGH TUH MAKE A GUY SICK!

IF IT WASN'T MUTINY, WE'D TEAR PETE APART AN' THROW HIM OVERBOARD! AN' YOU WITH HIM!
GOSH! YA WOULD?

OH, BOY! WHOOPEE! HOT DIGGETTY DOG!
WALT DISNEY

MINNIE, WHEN I LOOKS AT YUH I GIT TUH THINKIN' BEE-YEAUTIFUL THOUGHTS— LIKE WILDFLOWERS, AN' HONEY-SUCKLES AN' TWITTERIN' BOIDIES!
!

YUH'RE LIKE A BREATH O' MOUNTAIN AIR, DRIFTIN' ACROST A FIELD O' SWEET-SMELLIN' DAFFYDILS!
!

I LOVES YUH, MINNIE! I LOVES YUH SO MUCH THAT IF YUH DON'T MARRY ME, I'LL--I'LL--
? ?

I'LL THROW YUH TO TH' BLOOMIN' SHARKS!!
4-2

WELL, HOW ABOUT IT? ARE YUH GONNA MARRY ME OR AM I GONNA FEED YUH TO THUH SHARKS?
I---
I--I-
!

MICKEY! WHAT'LL I DO?
YA GOTTA SAY YES, MINNIE! YA JUST GOTTA!

WHADDAYA SAY, APPLE-BLOSSOM? HOW SOON SHALL WE GIT MARRIED?
I DON'T KNOW! I- I--I-

LISSEN, GAL! ARE YUH STALLIN' FER TIME? 'CAUSE IF YUH ARE---!
OH, NO, PETE! I'M JUST--- JUST---- OHHHH! BOO-HOO-HOOOOO!
4-6

MMMM---
!
!
4-5
© 1934, by Walt Disney Enterprises. Great Britain rights reserved

SMACK! SMACK! SMACK!

OHHHHH! SWEETIE! AIN'T LOVE GR-RAND?

POOR LI'L BUTTERFLY! SHE'S SO CRAZY TUH MARRY ME THAT SHE'S CRYIN' ABOUT IT!
SNIFF! SNIFF! SNIFF!
© 1934, by Walt Disney Enterprises. Great Britain rights reserved

WELL, CHEER UP KID! I WON'T KEEP YUH WAITIN' NO LONGER! WE'LL GIT MARRIED RIGHT NOW!
!
WALT DISNEY

COME ON YUH SWABS! ME AN' MINNIE'S GITTIN' MARRIED IN MY CABIN -- RIGHT NOW!
!
!

THUH BIG SLAB O' PORK! CAN'T WE DO NUTHIN' ABOUT IT?
NOT A CHANCE! IT'D BE MUTINY!

WELL — HERE WE ARE! YOU'LL BE TH WITNESSES! LET'S GIT STARTED!
BUT- BUT PETE! WHERE'S TH' MINISTER?

MINISTER? WHY - - I - - - UH - -
- - WELL, I'LL BE A BLANKETTY-BLANK SO-AN'-SO! I CLEAN FORGOT ABOUT THAT!
!

OHHHH! WOT'LL I DO? THUH POOR GAL HAD HER LITTLE HEART SET ON MARRYIN' ME!
!
© 1934, by Walt Disney Enterprises, Great Britain rights reserved

THE BIG SLAB O' PORK! HE AIN'T FITTEN TO MARRY A RATTLESNAKE!
I'D KILL HIM SOONER THAN LET HIM GET AWAY WITH IT, MUTINY OR NO MUTINY!

PETE! I'VE GOT IT! WHEN PEOPLE WANT TO GET MARRIED AT SEA, THE CAPTAIN CAN MARRY 'EM, CAN'T HE?
SURE! BUT---.
?

WELL-- YOU'RE THE CAPTAIN, AREN'T YA?
YOU'RE RIGHT! WHOOPEE! LET THUH WEDDIN' GO ON!
4-9

GIT READY FER THUH WEDDIN', HONEY-BLOSSOM! I'M CAPTAIN AN' CAPTAINS CAN MARRY FOLKS AT SEA!
!
!
!

!
?
SAY, PETE, I JUST THOUGHT O' SOMETHIN'! A CAPTAIN CAN'T MARRY HIMSELF! EVEN A MINISTER CAN'T DO THAT!

AWW WHY'D YUH HAFTA THINK O' DAT? NOW WOT'LL I DO? WOT'LL I DO?
LET ME THINK, NOW--- LET ME THINK--

?
!
?
?
!
PETE! WHY DON'T YA MAKE ME CAPTAIN LONG ENOUGH TO MARRY YA?
WALT DISNEY
4-10

MICKEY HAS BEEN MADE TEMPORARY CAPTAIN OF THE SMUGGLING SHIP, SO THAT HE CAN MARRY PEGLEG PETE AND MINNIE!

PEGLEG PETE HAS MADE ME CAPTAIN UNTIL HE IS MARRIED AND UNTIL THAT TIME, MY WORD IS LAW!

THEREFORE, AS CAPTAIN OF THIS SHIP, I HEREBY PRONOUNCE THAT— — — —

HE NEVER WILL GET MARRIED! THROW HIM IN IRONS!
WALT DISNEY
4.12

WHADDA YUH MEAN, "THROW ME IN IRONS" YUH LITTLE RAT!
YOU HEARD ME! I'M CAPTAIN, AN' THE ORDER STANDS, THROW HIM IN IRONS, BOYS!

NO, YUH DON'T! GIT OUTA MY WAY!

DOWN INTO THE HOLD AFTER HIM, MEN! HE CAN'T GET AWAY!
4.13

WE'VE GOT HIM!
LEMME OUT!
YEAH! AN' IT'S FOR MUTINY NOW!

HOIST HIM UP, MEN! WE'LL LET HIM COOL OFF A BIT!
MICKEY, YOU WERE WONDERFUL! I'M- - - ASHAMED OF MYSELF FOR DOUBTING YOU- - EVEN FOR A MINUTE!
AW! SHUCKS, MINNIE! DON'T WORRY ABOUT THAT! ONLY YOU SHOULD HAVE KNOWN I'D NEVER GO BACK ON YOU!
4.14
WALT DISNEY

THE MERMAID SAT ON THE CAPTAIN'S HAT! YO! HO! BLOW THE MAN DOWN!
THE LITTLE BRAT, SHE SQUASHED IT FLAT! YO! HO! BLOW THE MAN DOWN!
EX-CAPTAIN'S CABIN

HOME AGAIN!
CAPTAIN MICKEY IS MET AT THE HARBOR BY THE COAST GUARD TO WHOM HE SENT A RADIOGRAM TELLING OF CAPTURING PEGLEG PETE'S OPIUM-LADEN SMUGGLING SHIP!
WE'LL HAVE THEM IN JAIL IN AN HOUR, MICKEY! YOU HAVE DONE A FINE SERVICE FOR YOUR COUNTRY!
FOR MY- - ? OH, YEAH - OH - WELL - I WAS KINDA DOIN' IT FOR MINNIE, TOO!

HORACE! CLARABELLE! WE'RE HOME!!
MICKEY! MINNIE! SAKES ALIVE! IT'S LIKE GAZING ON THE DEAD! WHERE HAVE YOU BEEN?
WHERE HAVE THEY BEEN? YA DON'T MEAN T' TELL ME THEY'VE BEEN AWAY SOMEWHERE!
4-16

SAKES ALIVE MICKEY! THE PAPERS ARE FULL OF STORIES ABOUT YOUR CAPTURING THE OPIUM SHIP!
AW SHUCKS! TH' PAPERS ARE ALWAYS PRINTIN' STUFF LIKE THAT! IT'S SILLY!
MICKEY MOUSE CAPTURES SMUGGLERS

IT SAYS: "DUE TO MICKEY'S TESTIMONY IN THEIR BEHALF, ALL MEMBERS OF THE CREW PLEADED GUILTY AND DREW LIGHT SENTENCES!
YEAH! THEY'RE NOT REALLY CRIMINALS--LIKE PEGLEG PETE!
MICKEY MOUSE CAPTURES SMUGGLER

WELL, WHAT HAPPENED TO PETE?
TH' JUDGE IS GONNA GIVE HIM AN---INDETERMINATE SENTENCE!
YOU MEAN, LIKE 1 TO 14 YEARS?
MICKEY MOUS CAPTURES SMUGGLERS

?
!
YEAH! ONLY THIS ONE IS FROM 100 YEARS TO LIFE!
MICKEY MOUSE CAPTURES SMUGGLERS
4-17

In this cacophonic publicity still, Mickey conducts the Disney retinue: Goofy (known at that time as Dippy Dawg), Clarabelle the Cow, Horace Horsecollar, the Three Little Pigs (who won Disney an Academy Award) and the Big Bad Wolf, Pluto, Minnie Mouse, The Wise Little Hen, and a very early Donald Duck.

Hawaiian Holiday, 1937

Almost from the very beginning, Mickey ventured into foreign climes. In "Hawaiian Holiday," he was joined by Minnie and Donald in a lush, tropical setting.

Mr. Mouse Takes a Trip, 1940

Pegleg Pete reappeared in this film as the train conductor who made Mickey's trip difficult. Inside that bulging suitcase was a very cramped Pluto the Pup, who should have been in the baggage car.

Mickey's Parrot, 1938

The story of "Mickey's Parrot" is almost self-evident from these photographs: a conflict arises between jealous Pluto and a mischievous parrot. Note the wonderful sense of depth in this cartoon.

The Mickey Mouse Phenomenon, 1930's

Above: Walt Disney poses with some of the thousands of Disney-inspired merchandise—whose license fees enabled the Studio to continue production, regardless of box office pressures.
Opposite above: In the 1930's, Disney included a note in the King Features' Mickey comic strip that children could write to him for autographed pictures of the Mouse. This deluge came in the morning's mail.
Below: Magazines *(right)* and movie posters *(left)* helped spread the word.

COLUMBIA PICTURES presents
MICKEY MOUSE
The World's Funniest Cartoon Character in
WILD WAVES
He Talks!
He Sings!
He Dances!
MICKEY MOUSE
HERE TODAY!
MICKEY MOUSE
IN HIS LATEST ROLLICKING LAFF RIOT
"MICKEY'S REVUE"
Produced by WALT DISNEY
A COLUMBIA PICTURE
hello folks!
COLUMBIA PICTURES PRESENTS
MICKEY MOUSE
in
THE MOOSE HUNT
Produced by WALT DISNEY

Mickey merchandise came in all varieties. Kay Kamen, the longtime licensor of Disneyana, regularly published a catalogue of all that was available.

Mickey music kept the world humming.

PUT MICKEY MOUSE IN YOUR LOBBY

and *Children Business* in Your BOX-OFFICE!

Every wise showman knows that the backbone of his gross is dependent on the volume of children business he does. Children talk about the picture, drag their parents in, and are the greatest movie audience in the world. The MICKEY MOUSE sculptured figure shown on this page, and illustrated as well in the lobby display section of this pressbook, is the official MICKEY MOUSE lobby fixture.

25% *discount on each display*

Through a special arrangement with United Artists Pictures Corporation we are offering this figure direct to the exhibitors at a saving of 25%—our regular price is $4.00 per display, 25% discount bringing the net price down to $3.00 each.

MICKEY MOUSE relief statuette is a startlingly attractive figure. The pants are red, buttons blue, shoes are orange, gloves a vivid yellow. There is an easel on the back so that you can stand it up in the lobby of your theatre or if desired, you can remove the easel and mount it against the wall.

On the left is shown an actual reproduction of a dealer's window in Norwich, New York, showing how the Norwich Knitting Company's products were displayed in this dealer's window. Featured in the center of the display you can see a MICKEY MOUSE sculptured figure.

Laminite . . .

Exclusive Paper Mache

THIS MICKEY MOUSE figure is made of Laminite (exclusive paper maché), perfected by Old King Cole, Inc. It will stand the onslaughts of rough wear and hard usage. To even further preserve the life of this display it can be varnished so that it can be used in front of your theatre or on the marquee.

Perfect for Merchant Displays . and Dept. Store Windows . . .

Many of the MICKEY MOUSE licencees as well as exhibitors have taken advantage of the smart appearance of this MICKEY MOUSE display. They know it attracts business and dresses windows as well, and is ideal for show rooms and department store window displays as well as for the exhibitors lobby.

Make good use of the coupon on the left. As soon as your order is received we will ship them promptly to you.

Kindly send me F.O.B. Canton

.... Mickey Mouse Displays

at $3.00 each ($4.00 less 25%)

OLD KING COLE, Inc.

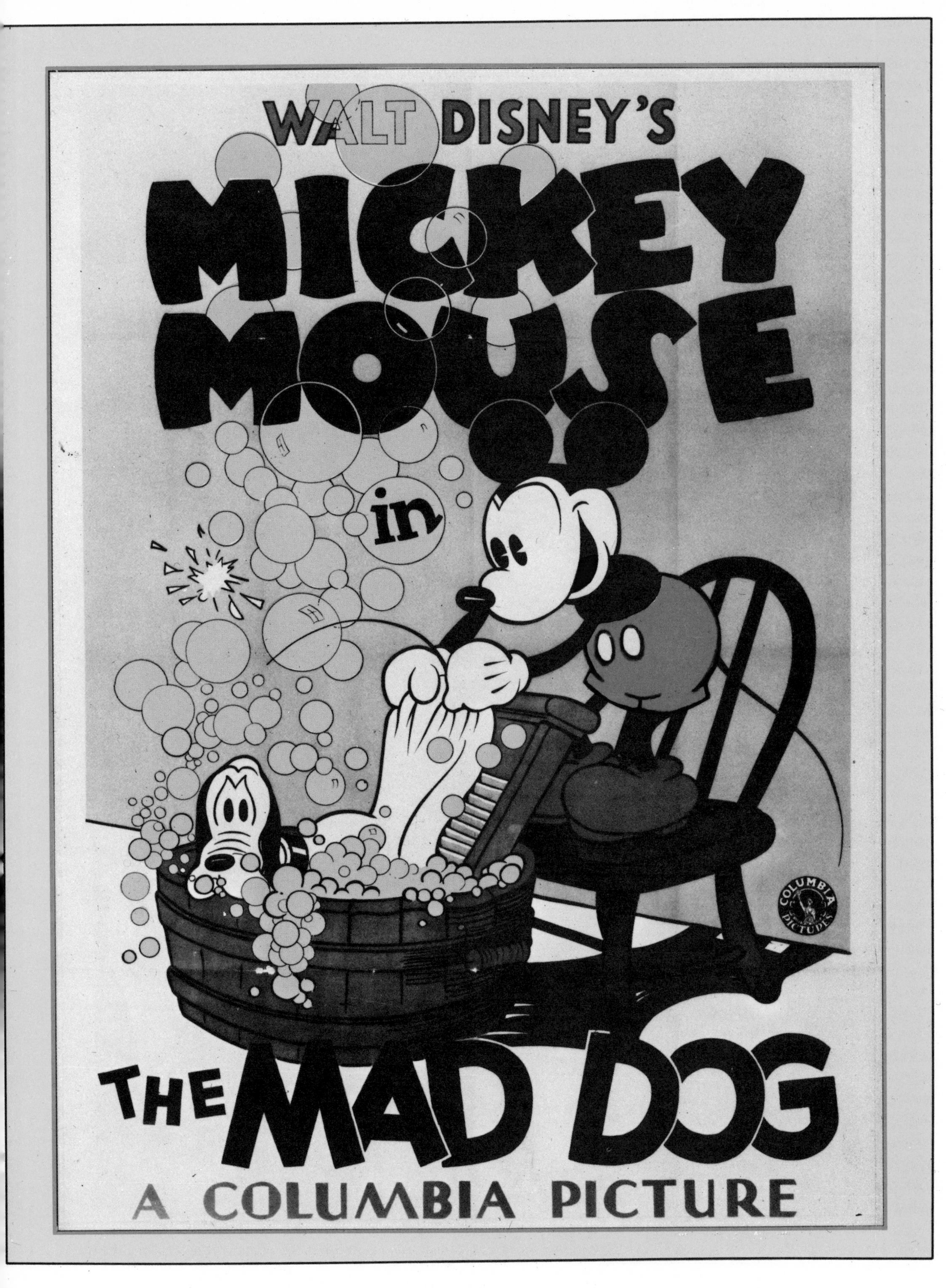
WALT DISNEY'S
MICKEY MOUSE
in
THE MAD DOG
A COLUMBIA PICTURE
COLUMBIA PICTURES

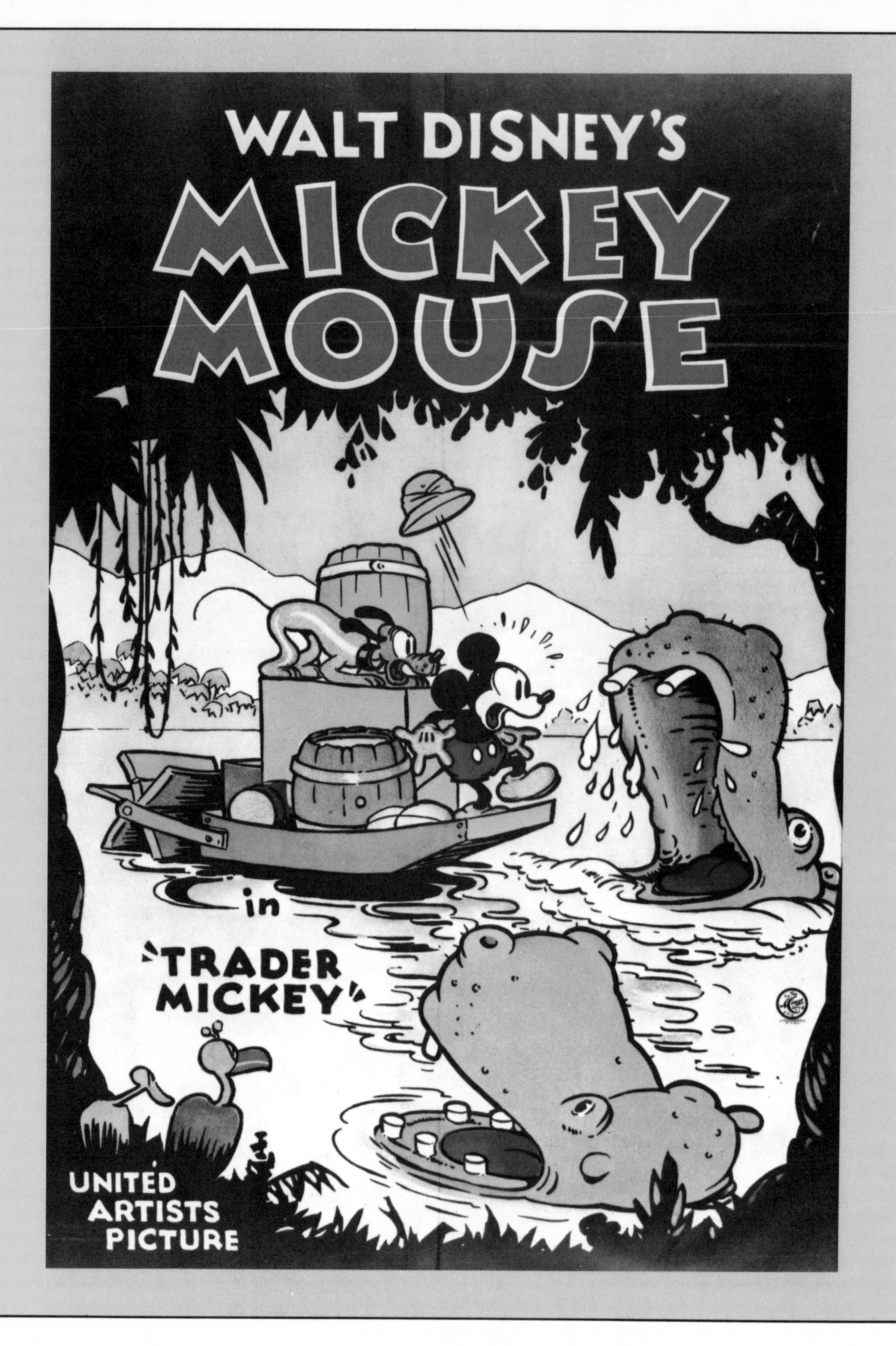
WALT DISNEY'S
MICKEY MOUSE
in
"TRADER MICKEY"
UNITED ARTISTS PICTURE

Above: One of the many projection devices available. It featured color slides of such films as "Gulliver Mickey," "Alpine Adventure," and several Silly Symphonies including "Santa's Workshop," "The Big Bad Wolf," and "The Three Little Pigs."
Left: a cheesecloth Mickey mask sports an infectious smile.

The Ingersoll Watch Company was a moribund Hartford manufacturer of timepieces when Kay Kamen sold the license for, as the patent described, "a time instrument comprising: a dial having time indicia thereon; rotatable seconds, minute and hour members; a figure mounted on said rotatable seconds member and fixed thereto so as to rotate therewith and simulating the body of an animate being; and a time indicator mounted on and rotatable with each of said rotatable minute and hour members and simulating a part of said animate being."

Above: The Watch: its many displays and sundry permutations.

The Ingersoll watch display in a Chicago department store.

Above: The Lionel Train Corporation was about to go under when someone came up with the idea of adding a rodent passenger to their toy trains. The corporation—needless to say—did not have to file for bankruptcy after all. Besides as a coal-stoker, Mickey could be had on a handcar, sharing the pumping with Minnie Mouse.
Opposite: Kay Kamen, the Disney licensor, produced a publicity release touting Mickey's eleventh-hour rescue.

THE NEW YORK TIMES,
TUESDAY, JANUARY 22, 1935.

Mickey Mouse Saves Jersey Toy Concern; Carries It Back to Solvency on His Railway

Special to THE NEW YORK TIMES.

NEWARK, N. J., Jan. 21.—Mickey and Minnie Mouse, pumping a red-painted hand car around a circular track before 253,000 Christmas trees this Winter, pulled the Lionel Corporation, Irvington toy manufacturers, back into the black, Federal Judge Guy L. Fake was told today.

After hearing the success story of the widely exploited cartoon characters, Judge Fake discharged equity receivers and turned assets of $1,900,000 back to the company. It was Mickey and Minnie's excur- ... let it be known that it had struck their fancy. Adults, whose perennial "kibitzing" on mechanical trains presumably bought for youngsters is a large factor in the trade, liked it, too. Stores hit upon it as a newspaper advertising leader and 253,000 were sold.

With each set of the car and tracks of the novelty, the company enclosed a circular picturing new streamlined electrical and mechanical trains, extolling ... similar-ties in enduran... to the handca... tional trackag...

NEW YORK WORLD-TELEGRAM,
MONDAY, JANUARY 21, 1935.

MICKEY MOUSE: HERO

He and Minnie Pulled Toy Firm Out of Red, Court Reveals.

Special to the World-Telegram.

NEWARK, Jan. 21.—Mickey and Minnie Mouse were praised in Federal Court today for the big part they played in ending the financial troubles of the Lionel Corp., makers of toys.

Mickey and Minnie did their share by pumping a handcar around thousands of toy Christmas railroad lines. Their good deed came to light today when Federal Judge Guy L. Fake discharged the Lionel Corp. from receivership, and praised the ...vers, Worcester Bouck and ... Frankel.

NEW YORK HERALD TRIBUNE,
JANUARY 22, 1935

Mickey Mouse Puts Bankrupt Firm on Its Feet

Handcar Riding Rodent and His Minnie Tow Lionel Corporation Out of Red

Court Compliments Pair

Says They Enabled Him to Terminate Receivership

Special to the Herald Tribune

NEWARK, N. J., Jan. 21.—Mickey and Minnie Mouse stepped down from the motion picture screen and received a pat on the back in United States District Court today, when their good deed in aiding in the rejuvenation of an ailing business was commented on by Judge Guy L. Fake.

With the assistance of Mickey and Minnie, the Lionel Corporation, make... ...ger Place, Irving... ...self out of receiv... ...onths. There were ...such as the good ...work in the ...d business ...part in the ...nie on a tin ...eeded spirit ... two Holly... brought to Judge Fake

Improving Our Railroads

A Federal court has just discharged from receivership one of the most celebrated, if not exactly the greatest, of American railway system... It is a road whose operations never affect t... car-loading statistics; no widows or orphans tremble for the fate of its financial struct... its traffic is almost wholly imaginary ... ules are erratic and its accident... ...mous. But there are few oldtim... ...road... will not be pleased ... th... company—which ... down ... thousands of scale ... in ... rooms, sitting ... the nation—has ...ed ... ies. For the Lionel company ha... up with the times. It went in for extensive electrification when the art was almost unknown on other roads; it has made constant improvements, and its widespread introduct... of the streamlined train is said to be ... sponsible for the success of ... principal credit, be... of genius ...

NEW YORK HERALD TRIBUNE
JANUARY 23, 1935

NEW YORK AMERICAN
TUESDAY, JANUARY 22, 1935

Mickey's Aid Ends Receivership

Mickey and Minnie Mouse, pumping a handcar around thousands of railroad lines during ... season, lifted the ... N. J., toy makers, ... out of receivership.

This was revealed in Federal Court at Newark yesterday when Judge Guy L. Fake discharged the company from receivership and praised the receivers.

Praising them for having paid claims of $296,197 and turning firm back to the court with as...

...of $1,900,000, he allowed the receivers, Worcester Bouck and Mandell Frankel fees of $20,000 and $7,500 respectively. Thomas N. McCarter, their counsel, was allowed $10,000.

It was termed probably the most successful receivership in the history of the Federal C...

Newark ... Bouck reveal... larity of ...

Mickey Mouse Saves Toy Firm With Minnie's Aid

THOSE joy-bringers of the films and the Daily and Sunday Mirror comic sections—Mickey and Minnie Mouse—got recognition yesterday in a Federal court which is stepping high even for Mickey and Minnie. Federal Judge Guy L. Fake called attention of the world to their good deed for the Lionel Corp., makers of toys, when he discharged that concern from receivership, "probably the most successful in the history of the Newark, N. J., court" and gave the bulk of credit to ...comic characters.

They had s... ceivers i... the firm ... Mick... handcar mostly du...

...chasers that the re... ...6,197 and turn ... $1,900,000.

...bit by pumping a toy ...ands of electric railroad lines, ...e Christmas shopping season.

DAILY MIRROR
Tuesday, January 22, 1935

Mickey Builds Solvency.

There can be only one name for the latest romance of business as recorded in Newark, N. J. The tale should be called The Lion and the Mickey Mouse. A $2,000,000 toy-manufacturing corporation has been hauled out of receivership and into full solvency by a miniature railroad-engine driven by a spring and operated by Mickey and Minnie. The new toy was devised by one of the company receivers for the Christmas holidays. It sold to the extent of 253,000 items. The direct profit plus the advertising for the rest of the company's line brought in enough to pay off $296,000 claims against the company...

...ptcy, ...nie, nibbled ...and set the prisoner ... DISNEY ought to make a new ...ure about the Newark affair, concluding with a triumphal dance by Mickey and his lady friend in honor of the Profit Motive.

THE NEW YORK TIMES,
WEDNESDAY, JANUARY 23, 1935

...Minnie made ...y late summer ...nufactured in ... shipped to dealers ... country. Christmas ...usual demand for the ... and more than 235,... were retailed for $1

...substantial profit on ...Bouck said, "and the ...into real money. W... on miles of track an... crossties. Mickey ... in putting the b... ...t. Streamline tr... ...rt. We had an... ...orld's Fair with ...y train built to ...ed overnight. ...eting the ... East...

But one n... Mr. Walt Dis... than streamli... out of bankru... railroads exper... Class I road s... Minnie Mice wou... people.

The Story of Mickey Mouse, 1930

Published in 1930 by the firm of Bibo & Lang, *The Story of Mickey Mouse* was originated by the eleven year old daughter of the publisher, Bobette Bibo.

UP in mouse fairyland, there was a big commotion. The mouse King was talking with the Prime Minister.

"Out he goes," said the King.

"Out who goes?" said the Prime Minister.

"Mouse number thirteen. The one who is always playing tricks and cutting capers."

The King summoned a page, and told him to bring mouse number thirteen to him. In a few minutes he was brought before the mouse King.

"I am very sorry, number thirteen, but you will have to leave Mouse Fairyland, because your pranks are too much for us."

All the time the King had been saying this, the mouse had been moving up closer and closer to the throne. Just as the King finished, number thirteen pulled the King's lower right whisker, the tenderest one in the King's beard.

"Ow!" roared the King. "Throw him out!"

The Prime Minister pushed the magic button and before number thirteen could say "Boo," out through the palace window he went, and he flew so fast it took his breath away, and after going hundreds and hundreds of miles, suddenly his body bumped against an airplane.

"Whew!" said he. "That was a close shave!"

He started to fall faster and faster, down and down, until all of a sudden, his

tail caught on the branch of a tree. He tried to get loose. To his surprise, the branch gave way, and he landed on a roof in Hollywood, California.

"Well, I might as well make the best of things. Let's see what's at the bottom of this chimney."

He slid down the inside of the chimney, and landed on a couple of logs. There at the bottom was a room. He started to explore for food. In back of a chair, there was a bag. As he was naturally an inquisitive little mouse, he wanted to see what was in the bag. He gnawed his way through and discovered a piece of old cheese, green with age. But number thirteen was so hungry that he broke off a piece and started to nibble at it. His spirits rose again, and he danced around the room. He did not notice the door open. A man stood in the doorway, watching the mouse's antics. He took his tail in his mouth and turned a somersault. He turned cart-wheels, stood on his head, and danced. Suddenly he turned around. He saw the man and started to run.

"Wait," said the gentleman, "Wait!"

Number thirteen looked at him and moved up a little closer.

"Who are you?" the little mouse asked.

"I am Walt Disney."

"Never heard of you."

"And who are you?" said Mr. Disney.

"I am mouse number thirteen. At least, that was my name in Mouse Fairyland."

"Tell me about yourself" said the gentleman.

So the mouse told him about his life. When he finished, Mr. Disney said:

"You give me an idea for a series of comedies. I have an idea that I can make you a picture star."

"Yeah?" said number thirteen.

"But first of all, we shall have to get you another name. Come, sit up here on the desk. What did you do when you first came to my house?"

"I ate old green cheese," said the mouse promptly.

"Now, let me see; green is the color of Ireland," said Mr. Disney, musingly. "Green, Irish, Mickey! I have it! Mickey Mouse shall be your name!"

And so this gentleman worked out an idea for little Mickey Mouse and several weeks later, Mickey found himself over at the studio, doing his tricks in front of directors, writers and camera-men. They decided to try him out. After a few comedies, the children began to want to see more of Mickey Mouse, and so he became a big star. Mr. Disney adopted him, and now he never eats any kind of cheese but that which is imported from Switzerland, and laughs when he thinks of that old green cheese he once ate. He also laughs with joy when he thinks of the luck it gave him; finding Mr. Disney and becoming a movie star. He has a little green roadster with his initials on it, M.M.D., Mickey Mouse Disney. Sometimes he takes his sweetheart, Minnie, out for a ride in it.

It's really a thrill to see Mickey and Minnie drive up to all the big picture openings in Hollywood. Sometimes Mickey walks into the theatre with Clara Bow or Mary Pickford, and Minnie is escorted by Buddy Rogers or other handsome movie stars. The people cheer when they see Mickey and his sweetheart, Minnie, and Oh! you should hear their little mouse squeaks of delight.

Mickey has a specially built cubby-hole in Mr. Disney's bedroom, but when he gets tired of his little cubby-hole, and Mr. Disney is asleep, he slips quietly out, and sneaks up on the foot of Mr-Disney's bed, where he snuggles down in the covers, and peacefully dreams.

THE END

The Birthday Party, 1931

"The Birthday Party" was dedicated "To all the little friends of Mickey Mouse throughout the world to whom he hopes to bring more happiness by coming into their homes," and signed by Walt Disney. This story, published by David McKay in Philadelphia in *Mickey Mouse Movie Stories*, was based on the cartoon short, "The Whoopee Party."

Mickey has his birthdays,
Just like other folks.
He celebrates in many ways,
Mostly playing jokes.

Today he went to Minnie's house,
To frolic and to play.
Did they have fun? Ask Mickey Mouse!
He won't forget THIS day!

TIPPING his straw hat at a rakish angle and twirling his brand new cane, Mickey Mouse gaily mounted the steps to Minnie's front porch.

He hadn't the slightest idea what was going on inside at that very minute. He didn't see the curtain on the front door move a wee bit, nor could he hear the excited whispering going on behind it.

Horsecollar Horace and Clarabelle Cow,
The lamb, the goat and the pig,
And chickens from the old hay mow
Were planning a party big.

They tried to find a place to hide,
No matter what its size,
Ere Mickey Mouse could get inside
And spoil the glad surprise.

Minnie was having a hard time trying to push the fat pig under the sofa, and finally seeing that it was a hopeless task, she threw the table cover over him and set the lamp on top of it.

Ting-a-ling, the old door bell
Echoed through the house,
Till Minnie, seeing all was well,
Greeted Mickey Mouse.

"OH, hello, Mickey!" "Hello, Minnie!" "How are you, Mickey?" "Oh, I'm fine, Minnie, and how are you?" "Just fine, Mickey, and how are you?" "Me? Oh—I'm just fine—and how are you?" "Oh, I'm fine, Mickey!" "Gee, that's good—then we're both fine!" said Mickey, and they both laughed, and Mickey stepped into the big living room.

"Surprise! SURPRISE!" They all jumped up—
The pigs, goats, ducks and chickens,
The cow and horse and little pup—
And shouted like the dickens!

They all joined hands and danced around him, and Mickey saw right away that he was in for a great celebration.

The cook, a big fat pig, came running in from the kitchen with a huge birthday cake, with candles on it. Now, as you know, it is the custom to let the one whose birthday it is blow out the candles. So Mickey took a deep breath and blew with all his might. And he blew so hard that all the frosting of the cake flew right into the cook's face. But it certainly was a wonderful cake and when it was cut up everybody enjoyed it to the last crumb.

And what was that big package, all wrapped up, over there in the corner? "Why—that's your birthday present, Mickey! Go on and open it!" cried Minnie, and—

Mickey ran across the room and looked at the package.

"Is it a joke?" he asked. And Minnie answered: "Why don't you open it, and see for yourself?"

So Mickey wasted no more time, and tore off the wrapping paper. And standing there, waiting to be played, was a tiny piano. He shouted for joy, then jumped up on the stool and ran his fingers over the keys.

Minnie, too, commenced to play
Along with Mickey Mouse,
While all began to dance and sway—
They fairly shook the house!

But Mickey and Minnie wanted to do a little dancing themselves, so they stopped playing and skipped out on the floor.

The piano stool then came to life,
And kept the music flowing,
Till joy and happiness were rife,
And everyone got going!

Gliding and sliding around the room,
On the carpet and through the door,
Mickey and Minnie went Ker-ZOOM!
And landed on the floor!

The pig's coat burst, his trousers split,
Which made him blush and cough.
And as he watched his chance to flit,
His torn pants came clear off!

But nobody paid any attention to the pig's trousers because they were all so busy singing and dancing themselves.

And then everybody stopped dancing and formed a great circle, while—

Horsecollar Horace and Clarabelle Cow
Started to dance—and they both knew how!
They stamped and shook, they shouted and tapped,
They wiggled and jiggled and clapped and slapped.

Slipping and tripping, as if by chance,
Over the parlor this merry pair slid.
Whoopee! You never have seen such a dance
As Horsecollar Horace and Clarabelle did!

Then suddenly Mickey spied the xylophone in the corner and rushing over, he seized the sticks and began to play.

Soon he was rolling the keys up in piles,
Letting them tumble back down.
He showed the folks all the fanciest styles,
And drummed like a circus clown.

And then the old xylophone started to prance,
So Mickey astride of him jumped.
He cavorted around with hop, skip and dance,
And bounded, and pounded and bumped.

But Mickey hung on to his musical steed
With a wave of his hand and a grin,
But the old xylophone put on all his speed
And Mickey lit KLUNK! on his chin!

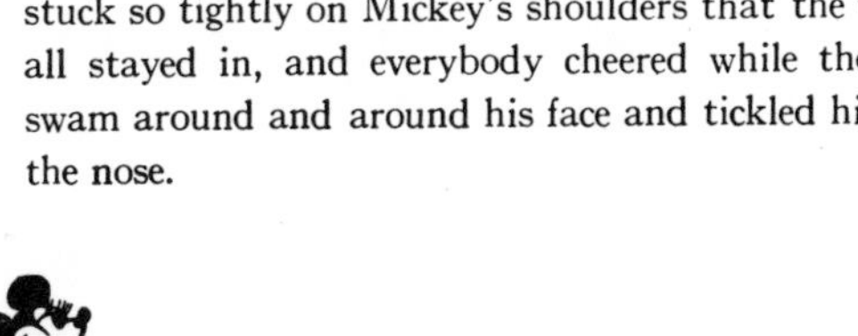

Yes—but what was worse—he hit the pedestal holding the goldfish bowl. And the bowl came CRASH! down over Mickey's head and stayed there. In fact, it stuck so tightly on Mickey's shoulders that the water all stayed in, and everybody cheered while the fish swam around and around his face and tickled him on the nose.

Gee, wouldn't it be glorious
If every day could be
A birthday just like Mickey's was
For folks like you and me?

Gulliver Mickey, 1934

In 1934 the Disney Studio released "Gulliver Mickey" as a cartoon short. Soon thereafter, it appeared in *Mickey Mouse Movie Stories, Book Two*, published by David McKay.

While his little nephews were playing around the living room in his house, Mickey Mouse sat in a big chair, reading "Gulliver's Travels." He loved to read books of adventure, for they stirred his imagination, and he always put himself in the hero's place. As he read, he could see himself doing all the things the story described—and more besides. Therefore, when the children tired of their play and asked him to tell them a story, Mickey laid his book aside and began to tell a fantastic tale that came partially from the book and partially from his own fertile imagination.

"It happened a long time ago," he said, "when I was just a little

bit older than you are. One dark and stormy night I was ship-wrecked and cast up on the beach. I didn't know where I was, and I was so tired from fighting the waves that I didn't care much. So I just stretched out and went sound asleep.

"Next morning, when I awoke, the storm had cleared up and the sun was shining, so I decided to explore a bit. But when I tried to sit up, I found I couldn't do it. I couldn't move a muscle. I was tied down, hand and foot, by dozens of strings that ran over my body and down to tiny stakes driven into the ground."

"Were ya scared?" asked one of his nephews.

"I was at first," Mickey answered, "but by turning my eyes a little I soon found out what had happened. I had been captured by an army of tiny little people just about as big as one of my fingers. And they had tied me down in a huge open court in the middle of their toy city.

"The streets were full of the little people, all of them jabbering at the tops of their funny, squeaky voices. They had never seen anybody like me, so they climbed up the ropes and crawled into my pockets, and walked back and forth all over me. It struck me funny and

I began to laugh. My tummy shook, like it always does when I laugh hard, and that broke all the strings that were holding me down. So I sat up and looked around me.

"All the little people ran away, 'cause they thought I might hurt them, or something. Then one very dignified, fat little fellow rode up on horseback and stopped beside me. I picked him up in my hand and held him out so that he could talk to me. He was awf'ly cute and so fat and funny and pompous that I couldn't help laughing. He unrolled a long scroll and began to read it, and his voice was very, VERY high and squeaky—a little tiny voice away up here—and of course that made me laugh harder than ever, 'cause he took himself so seriously.

"Naturally I couldn't understand a word he said, and he was so dignified and majestic that I thought I'd have some fun with him. So while he was giving his speech I rocked my hand, and bent my fingers and tickled him in the ribs. It made him furious, and when I put him down on the ground he shouted something to the other people and they started into action.

"I guess he was a general, or something, and he must have given orders to the army, 'cause out of a little fort ran a whole lot of soldiers pulling the cutest little cannons you ever saw. They aimed 'em at me and started firing. Of course, they didn't hurt me much—I was so big, you see—but they did sting a little. So I got up and began to back away.

"It was a lot of fun, and they were all so very serious and brave that I wouldn't have hurt any of 'em for anything in the world. I had to be careful not to step on any of them as I headed for the ocean. But I finally made it, dodging the little bullets as I went.

"I waded out in the water up to my knees and then looked around. Coming toward me, around a nearby point, was the entire fleet—the cutest little boats you ever saw in your life. They were about as big as those ship models Uncle Mortimer used to make, and they were all quaint old fashioned boats—schooners with bright-colored sails, galleys with long sweeping oars, and all of them manned by the tiny people. They meant business, too, for they came as fast as they could sail, all of them armed to the teeth and all of the guns aimed right at me.

"When they got within range, which was about ten feet, they started

firing. The bullets stung me a little, like the ones in town did, but of course they didn't really hurt at all. So I went over and picked up one of the boats. Just as I did, the cannon in front went off and the bullet hit me right in the nose. That did hurt, for the cannon was only about a foot away. So when they loaded it again, I stuck my finger in the mouth of it, and when it went off it exploded.

"The poor sailors were almost scared to death, and they jumped overboard and started swimming for their lives. I didn't want to hurt 'em, of course, so I put the boat back in the water and scooped up all the sailors and very carefully placed them on the deck again. Then I blew on the sail and splashed water on the side of the boat so it would have to go away and not bother me any more. I was having such a good time with it that I didn't notice a galley speeding up behind me. I was stooped over looking at the sailboat when WHAM! the galley smacked me. I was so surprised that I let out a wild yell and jumped clear out of the water and up on land again.

"All the people began to cheer, for they thought they had me on the run. And they began to bring out more cannons and guns and

giant bows and arrows and horses and all kinds of things. I couldn't dodge 'em all, of course, for there were too many of them. So I bent over and tried to cover my eyes, because that was the only place they could possibly have hurt me. And I was laughing so hard I couldn't have run anyway, so all I could do was just let 'em shoot to their hearts' content.

"While I had my eyes all covered up to protect them, the shooting suddenly stopped. And instead of the popping of guns, I heard a lot of terrified shouting. The people seemed scared of something. I thought they might be playing a trick on me, trying to get me to expose myself or something, so I peeked out to see what was going on. And I saw that it was no trick. They were really scared. I couldn't understand it, for they had been so brave up to then. So I stood up to see what I had done to frighten them. And then I saw it! Coming along toward me, crawling over their houses and buildings, was the biggest spider that ever walked! He was almost half again as big as I was! And he was coming straight toward me, his face drawn in a ferocious growl of rage.

"No wonder the little people were scared. I was scared plenty myself. But the way to win a fight is to pitch right in and get it over with before the other fellow knows it's even started. So I jumped at the spider and let him have it with both fists. I socked him with my right, then my left, then my right and then my left. And then I uppercut him on the chin. He was wobbling and staggering, so I grabbed him by the legs and threw him clear out in the ocean. And that was the end of the spider."

"Is it the end of the story too?" asked one of his nephews.

"Yes, that's all there is," replied Mickey. "And what's more, anybody who doesn't believe it owes me a dime."

Without a word, all his nephews filed out of the room. At the door one of them turned and held out his hand. Mickey shook it gravely, and the little fellow left the house. Then Mickey stopped, puzzled, and looked at his outstretched hand.

In it was a shiny new dime!

The Sorcerer's Apprentice, 1940

Fantasia (1940) was a triumph of art and imagination for the Disney Studio. Comprised of seven pieces which ranged from abstract visual interpretations of music to animated ballet, the film grew out of a 1938 plan to produce Mickey in "The Sorcerer's Apprentice." Leopold Stokowski came on as conductor, and persuaded Disney to expand his idea in a daring and ambitious way.

Mickey is a hard-working apprentice to a mighty magician, and toils long hours while the Sorcerer casts spells and concocts potions.

The Sorcerer heads for his sleeping quarters after a long session of magic-making, and leaves his powerful cap behind.

With Mickey's supervision gone, his mischievous nature surfaces, as he eyes his master's cap.

'he temptation to try on the magic cap is too much for /lickey to resist. He feels a glow of power...

...and decides to test his new power on a very mundane task—water carrying. With one magic gesture his broom comes to life! "Now! That's what I call a job well done!"

Mickey is naturally relieved to be left without his chores.

His laziness overcomes him...

...as he falls asleep to dream of great feats of magic.

He wakes with a start to discover that the broom has flooded out his master's study. Mickey attempts to stop the broom!

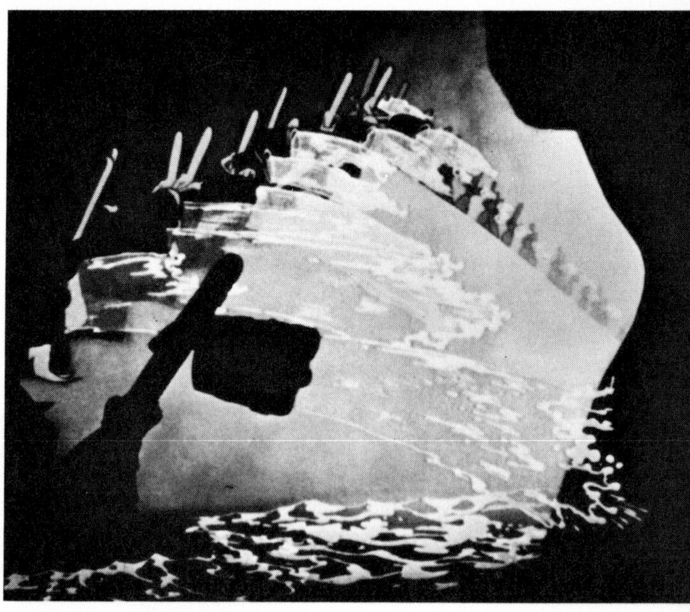

He splinters his helper with an axe, but the pieces leap up—each a broom, each carrying water. What a dilemma! How will he ever get out of this one?

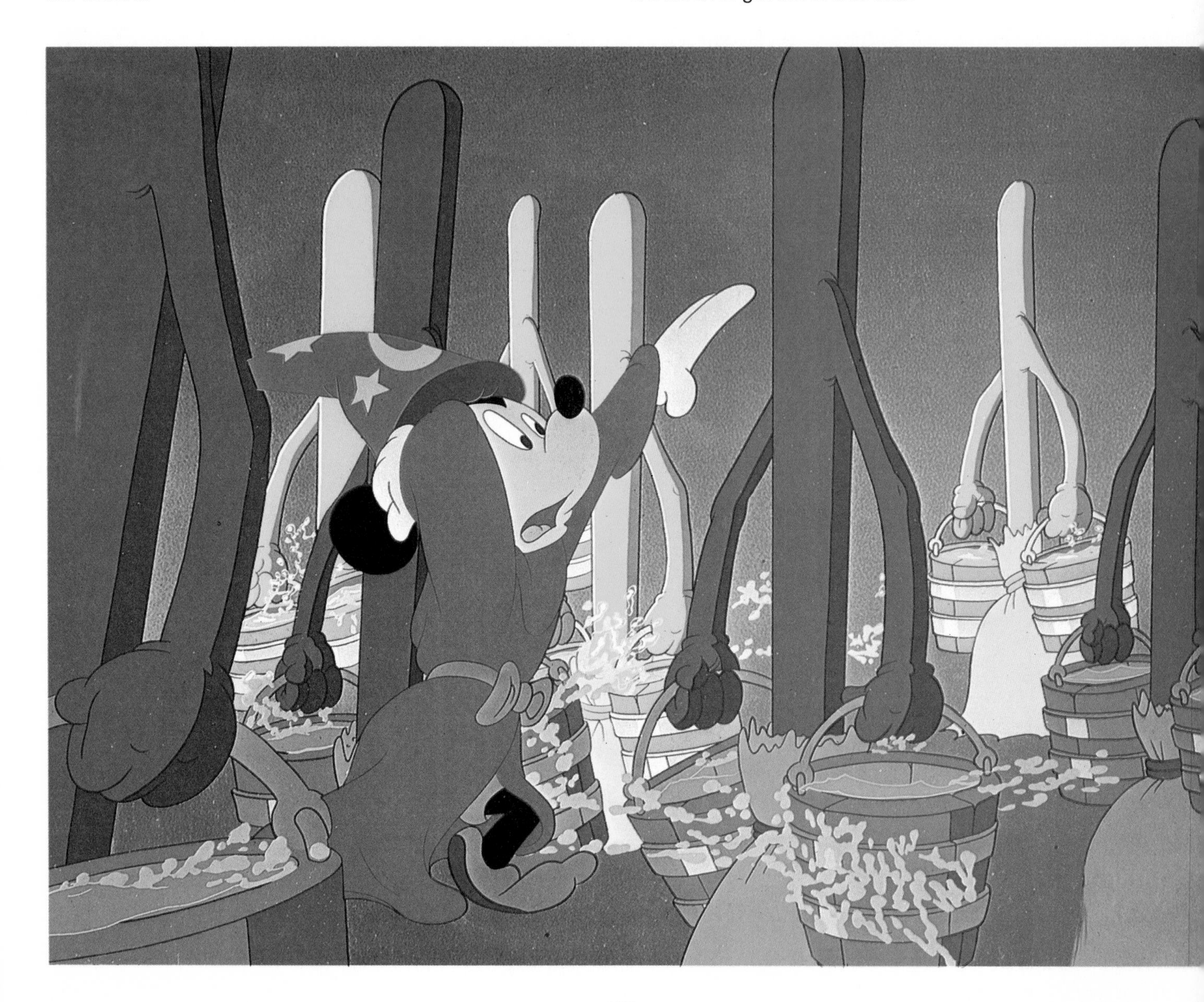

The deluge swallows up poor Mickey and he scrambles to relative safety onto the Sorcerer's book of spells.

At this moment, the mighty Sorcerer returns and with one imperious gesture rolls back the waves. He looks with patience and much amusement at his little apprentice .... as we leave them to each other.

The Sunday Comics, 1946–1968

The Sunday Mickey Mouse comic page began running in the early Thirties, and eventually reached an American audience of 15 million readers. This selection begins in 1946 and continues through 1968, and was drawn by Manuel Gonzalez and written by Bill Walsh (until 1963) and Roy Williams (through 1968). (It is interesting to note that the latter two were involved in the Mickey Mouse Club series in the Fifties—an excellent demonstration of the ways the Studio utlilized people.) The Sunday comics frequently featured Minnie, Mickey's pal Goofy, and Pluto, plus one or two nephews of Mickey's, named Morty and Ferdie. Very often the entire story would be given over to the adventures of one of these subsidiary characters.

Until the daily strips resumed their gag-a-day format in 1955, these Sunday stories portrayed Mickey in his most contemporary manner.

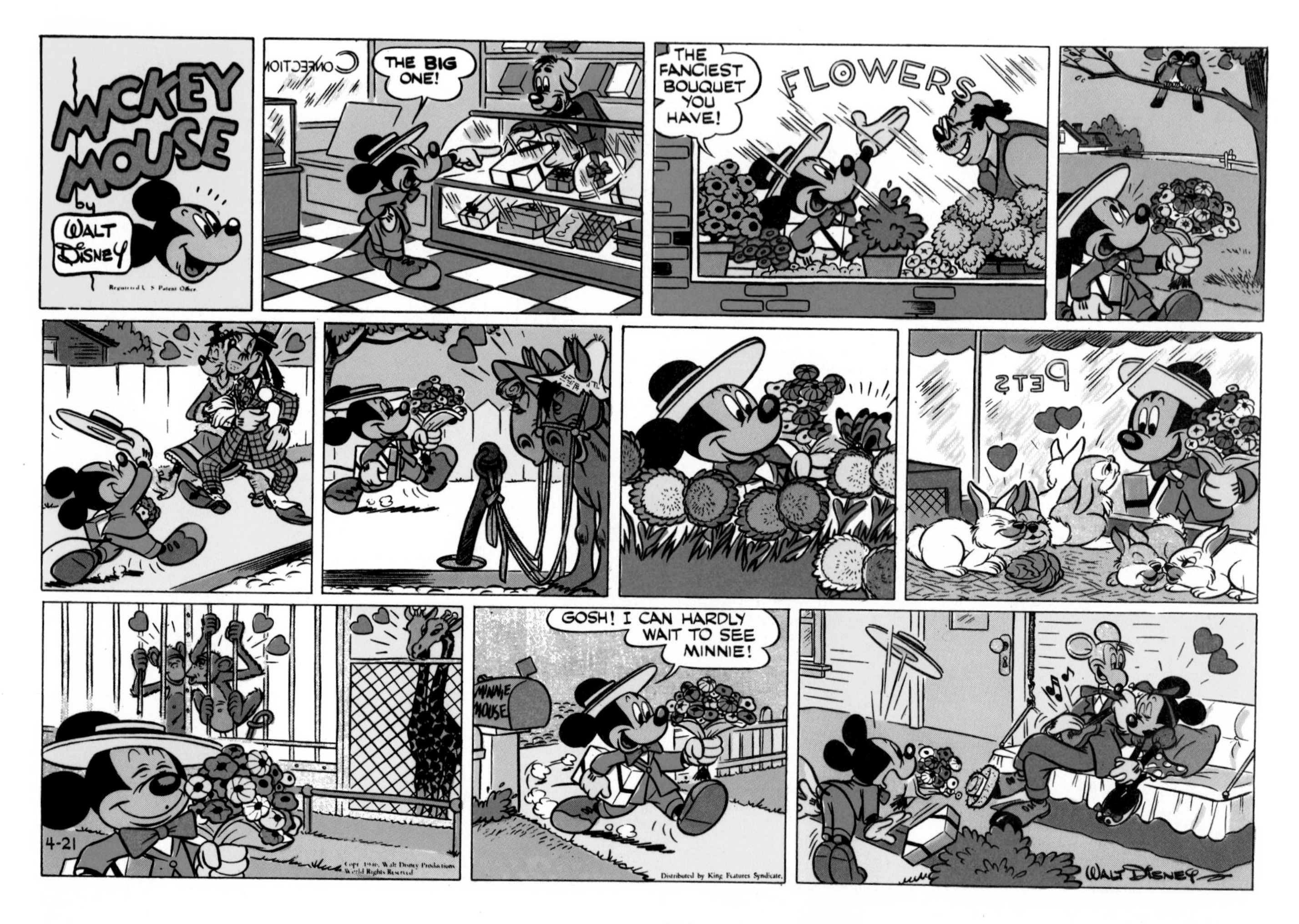

MICKEY MOUSE
by
WALT DISNEY
Registered U. S. Patent Office

REMEMBER, GOOFY... WE'RE DEPENDING ON YOU!
DON'T WORRY, MICKEY!
GOAL

GOAL
CRACK

HURRAH!
GREAT PLAY
YEA-BO

GOAL

SOCK

WHATA GUY!
YEA
TEAM! TEAM!
GOOD WORK, GOOFY!
PAT PAT
CLAP! CLAP!

GOAL

GOAL
1-25
World Rights Reserved

IS THERE A CAN OPENER IN THE HOUSE?
GOAL
Distributed by King Features Syndicate
WALT DISNEY

MICKEY MOUSE
by
WALT DISNEY

IS IT TRUE YOU'RE DOING A TELEVISION SHOW, GOOFY?
YUP! THEY WANT ME TO DO MUH TRAVELOGUE MOVIES!

GOOD LUCK, GOOFY! I'LL BE WATCHING!
SWELL!

GAWRSH! I GOTTA HURRY! IT'S ALMOST TIME FOR MUH FIRST SHOW!

T.V. STUDIO
STATION WOW
THUH TRAVELOGUE FILM! I FORGOT IT! AND I AIN'T GOT TIME TO GO HOME!

WHY DID IT HAVE TO HAPPEN ON MUH VERY FIRST SHOW!

SAILORS' CAFE
CHECKS CASHED

...AND NOW WE APPROACH THUH TROPICAL ISLE OF LINGA-LONGA.....
11-12
Copr. 1950, Walt Disney Productions
World Rights Reserved

...AND AS THUH SUN SETS ON LINGA-LONGA... WE SAY FAREWELL TO THUH NATIVES!
Distributed by King Features Syndicate

THANKS, FELLAS! YUH SAVED MUH LIFE!
WALT DISNEY

MICKEY MOUSE
by
WALT DISNEY

PLUTO! IF YOU DON'T STOP DRAGGING JUNK HOME ALL THE TIME...

BRR... WHERE DID YOU GET THIS?

WELL... GET IT OUT OF HERE! IT MAKES ME NERVOUS!

THERE HE GOES... DIGGING UP THE YARD AGAIN!

PLUTO!
PAT PAT

ANOTHER THING... STOP TEARING UP THE YARD! YOU'VE GOT THINGS BURIED ALL OVER THE PLACE!

REMEMBER... NO MORE DIGGING... UNDER ANY CIRCUMSTANCES! DO WE UNDERSTAND EACH OTHER?
UFF!
7-13
Copr. 1952, Walt Disney Productions World Rights Reserved
Distributed by King Features Syndicate.

GOSH! THAT'S THE THING PLUTO...
PRICELESS ART OBJECT MISSING
THROWN INTO MUSEUM TRASH BY MISTAKE!
$500 REWARD OFFERED FOR RETURN!

THAT NIGHT
PLUTO, PLEASE... I GIVE YOU PERMISSION TO DIG IT UP! ER... AT LEAST SHOW ME WHERE IT IS!
WALT DISNEY

MICKEY MOUSE
by
WALT DISNEY

COME ON, MICKEY! I'VE GOT SHOPPING TO DO!
OH, NO!
DEPT. STORE

IT'S A TRAP TO MAKE ME CARRY DOZENS OF BUNDLES!
GO ON, SILLY!

I PROMISE YOU WON'T HAVE TO CARRY ANY OF MY PACKAGES!
THAT'S A DEAL!

LADIES' DEPT.
I'LL JUST BROWSE AROUND!
YOU DON'T EVEN HAVE TO COME IN HERE! I'LL MEET YOU AT THE ENTRANCE!

GOSH... HOW WOMEN LOVE TO SHOP!

AISLE A
INTERESTING GADGET!
JIFFY CAN OPENER $5.00
KITCHEN AND HARDWARE DEPT.
SALE

TIME TO MEET MICKEY!
8-26
Distributed by King Features Syndicate.

FOR GOODNESS' SAKE! WHAT'S KEEPING HIM?

ER... MINNIE... I WONDER IF YOU COULD GIVE ME A HAND WITH THESE!
WALT DISNEY

MICKEY MOUSE
by
WALT DISNEY

MORTY!

LOOKS LIKE THERE'S A WAR GOING ON!
BUILDING BLOCKS

MIND IF I PLAY?
OKAY!

GOSH, UNCA MICKEY... YOU'VE WRECKED MY CASTLE!

RELAX, MORTY, IT'S ONLY PLAY!

HERE... I'LL REBUILD IT FOR YOU!
OKAY!

LOOK, MORTY... ISN'T IT BEAUTIFUL?
6-23
© 1957 Walt Disney Productions World Rights Reserved

WHEE!
CRASH
Distributed by King Features Syndicate.

GEE, UNCA MICKEY... IT'S ONLY PLAY!
WALT DISNEY

MICKEY MOUSE
by
WALT DISNEY

WHAT A GLORIOUS DAY FOR A PICNIC!
I CAN'T WAIT FOR THAT LUNCH YOU PACKED, MINNIE!

HERE'S A NICE SPOT!

BOY! LOOK AT THAT CAKE!

HEY!
MY CAKE!

YOU BIG HULKING BRUTE! YOU SHOULD BE ASHAMED OF YOURSELF!

MINNIE... BE CAREFUL!
THE VERY IDEA! STEALING THINGS THAT BELONG TO OTHER PEOPLE! YOU'RE NOTHING BUT A COMMON THIEF!
Distributed by King Features Syndicate.

LATER
LOOK! HE MUST HAVE STOLEN THAT TOO!
BEANS
622

GUESS HE'S GOING BACK FOR MORE!
© 1958 Walt Disney Productions World Rights Reserved

MINNIE, YOU'VE REFORMED HIM! I ALWAYS DID SAY YOU HAD A GIFT FOR WORDS!
FLOUR
BEANS
WALT DISNEY

MICKEY MOUSE
by
WALT DISNEY

PUBLIC SCHOOL 12

BICYCLE SH
JET RACER $50

STRAIGHTENING UP YOUR ROOM? YOU?
I LIKE THINGS NEAT EV'RY NOW AND THEN!

HMMM...
I HAVE A LITTLE SPARE TIME! THOUGHT I'D GIVE YOUR SHOES A POLISH!

I THINK I'M BEGINNING TO GET THE IDEA!

JUST AS I THOUGHT! YOU'VE BEEN BUTTERING UP TO ME BECAUSE YOU'VE GOT A BAD REPORT CARD!
BUT, UNCA MICKEY...
1-11

ALL "A'S"! GOSH! MORTY... I'M SORRY!
REPORT CARD
ARITHMETIC A
HISTORY A
SPELLING A
SCIENCE A
GEOGRAPHY A
LANGUAGE A
© 1959 Walt Disney Productions World Rights Reserved

LATER
YOU SURE KNOW HOW TO HANDLE YOUR UNCA MICKEY!
WALT DISNEY
Distributed by King Features Syndicate.

MICKEY MOUSE
by
WALT DISNEY

HUH?
MEOW! MEOW!

GOSH, LIZA BELLE-- YOU DON'T LOOK SO GOOD!

YEAH--DOC! BETTER COME ON OVER!

SHE DOESN'T LOOK WELL, AND THAT'S A FACT!

I'LL KEEP HER WITH ME OVERNIGHT!
DON'T WORRY, LIZA BELLE! I'LL TAKE CARE OF YOUR LITTLE ONES!

HEY!

PICK ON SOMEONE YOUR SIZE!

BEAT IT!
10-9
Distributed by King Features Syndicate.

STOP SHAKING THE BRANCH, WILL YOU?
© 1960 Walt Disney Productions World Rights Reserved

NEXT MORNING
IS SHE BETTER?
YES! YOU CAN TAKE HER HOME NOW!
OFF HOU 8-5

YOU GO HOME, LIZA BELLE! I'M STAYING HERE!

MICKEY MOUSE
by
WALT DISNEY

?
!
SPLAT

OH-OH! RAIN!
© 1961
Walt Disney Productions
World Rights Reserved

QUICK, MICKEY! GET THE TOP UP!

HURRY!

URRGH-H!

WE'VE GOT TO GET OUT OF THIS!
7-23

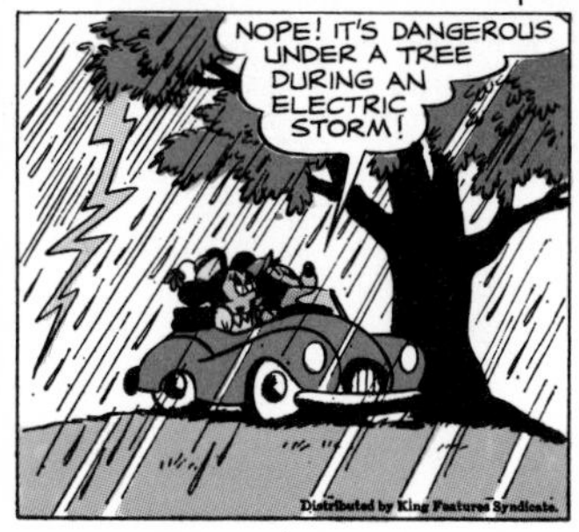
NOPE! IT'S DANGEROUS UNDER A TREE DURING AN ELECTRIC STORM!
Distributed by King Features Syndicate.

!

MICKEY MOUSE
by
WALT DISNEY

?
MEE-OWW!

MEE-OWW!

YOU POOR LITTLE THING!

...AND THE POOR LITTLE CREATURE IS STUCK IN THE TREE, MICKEY!
MEE-OWW!

GOSH--I'VE GOT AN IMPORTANT MEETING FIRST THING IN THE MORNING... BUT...

MEE-OWW!
PLEASE BE CAREFUL!

SPTT...
YOU'RE FRIGHTENING HIM!
Distributed by King Features Syndicate.

CRACK
THUMP

MICKEY MOUSE

© 1962
Walt Disney Productions
World Rights Reserved

MEE-OWWW...

MICKEY MOUSE
by
WALT DISNEY

PIANOS
SALE PLAYER PIANOS
BOY!

I'VE ALWAYS LOVED THESE PLAYER PIANOS!

I'LL SURPRISE MINNIE AND CLARABELLE WITH A CONCERT!

I'LL TRY THIS OUT BEFORE MINNIE AND CLARABELLE GET HERE!
© 1965 Walt Disney Productions World Rights Reserved

OOPS!

WHOA!

HALP!

MICKEY SAID HE HAD A SURPRISE FOR US!
WONDER WHAT!
RING
4-21
Distributed by King Features Syndicate.

RING
MMPFF!

IF THIS IS ONE OF HIS JOKES!
RING
KNOCK KNOCK

JUST LET HIM TRY TO TALK HIS WAY OUT OF THIS ONE!
MMPH! MMPH!

MICKEY MOUSE
by
WALT DISNEY

ELECTRIC EYE
FOR YOUR GARAGE DOOR!
AUTOMATIC
HMMM!

OOF!

WHY DON'T YOU LOOK WHERE YOU'RE GOING?

IT'S AN ELECTRIC EYE FOR THE GARAGE DOOR!
TOOLS

LATER

SLAM
?

© 1965 Walt Disney Productions World Rights Reserved

BAM
2-7

BOOM
SOMETHING'S GOTTA GO! EITHER YOUR PETS OR MY ELECTRIC EYE!

GAWRSH! THANKS, MICKEY!
Distributed by King Features Syndicate

MICKEY MOUSE
by
WALT DISNEY

WHO'S MAKING THAT NOISE?
UNCA MICKEY-SINGING!
DARTS

DOES HE DO IT ALL THE TIME?
ONLY ON SPECIAL OCCASIONS...

...LIKE WHEN HE HAS A DATE WITH MINNIE!

HI, MILLIE! IS MINNIE READY?
NOT QUITE...
Distributed by King Features Syndicate.

...BUT SHE WON'T BE LONG!
MY! WHAT A CUTE DOLL!

OH, I'VE GOT LOTS MORE, BUT...SHHH!
SHHH?

THEY'RE SLEEPING!
© 1966
Walt Disney Productions
World Rights Reserved

LATER
YOU CAN TELL MICKEY I'M READY NOW!
11-27

BUT BEFORE WE LEAVE, PUT ALL YOUR DOLLS AWAY!
ALL BUT ONE OF THEM!

WHY NOT ALL OF THEM?

BECAUSE ONE IS YOURS!
!
?
ZZZ
WALT DISNEY

WALT DISNEY'S
MICKEY MOUSE

I'M SENTIMENTAL TONIGHT! LET'S PLAY SOME OLD RECORDS!

SHALL WE USE THE OLD PHONOGRAPH?

I'M NOT THAT SENTIMENTAL!

LISTEN TO THIS!
Distributed by King Features Syndicate.

MEMORY LANE GIRL OF MY DREAMS

HOW WONDERFUL TO LOOK BACK ON THE BEAUTIFUL SONGS OF OUR YESTERDAYS!
YES!

MUSIC SHOP
NOW-LISTEN TO THIS ONE!
© 1967
Walt Disney Productions
World Rights Reserved

I AM A YARD OF WEEDS, A YARD OF WEEDS...YES, I AM...YES I AM...A YARD OF WEEDS
UGH..!
31

GROOVY!
I AM A YARD OF WEEDS...

A YARD OF WEEDS
HOW AWFUL!

I AM A YARD OF WEEDS...
WHAT WILL MORTY'S GENERATION HAVE TO LOOK BACK ON?
TOP TEN

WALT DISNEY'S
MICKEY MOUSE

DOCTOR PROCTOR
NOTHING SERIOUS- YOU'RE JUST TOO TENSE!

THIS SHOULD FIX YOU UP!

"VISIT GOOFY'S JOKE SHOP!"
Rx

ANYTHING SPECIAL, MICKEY?
NO, JUST CAME IN TO BROWSE!
GOOFY'S JOKE SHOP
BARKING DOGS $1.25

TRICK CAMERA
WHAM
© 1967
Walt Disney Productions
World Rights Reserved

SQUIRT
SQUIRT FLOWER
59¢ each

AH-CHOO
SNEEZE POWDER

TRICK GOLF CLUBS
GULP

SPLAT
"POPPING" CORK BOTTLES
5-7

YIPE
JACK IN THE BOX

THAT'S ENOUGH BROWSING FOR ONE DAY!
GOOFY'S JOKE SHOP
Distributed by King Features Syndicate.

WALT DISNEY'S
MICKEY MOUSE

I'VE GOT TO CALL ALVIN, BUT MY WALKIE-TALKIE ISN'T WORKING!

NEITHER IS OUR HOT LINE!

I'LL HAVE TO USE THE OLD-FASHIONED PHONE!

IS ALVIN THERE?
SORRY, MORTY...

...HE'S TAKING A SHOWER BREAK!
Distributed by King Features Syndicate.

IS MILLIE THERE?

SHE'S TAKING A NAP BREAK!

ACME PRODUCTS INC.
IS UNCA MICKEY THERE?
3-17

HE'S TAKING A TEA BREAK!

I'M TAKING A DO-NOTHING BREAK!
CLICK
© 1968
Walt Disney Productions
World Rights Reserved

Clock Cleaners, 1937

ade in 1937, "Clock Cleaners" is a good example of how Mickey was
adually giving his cartoon pre-eminence over to his pals—in this case,
onald Duck and Goofy. "Clock Cleaners" featured some Harold
oyd-inspired cliffhanging.

Fun & Fancy Free, 1947

Fun and Fancy Free (1947) was a melange of live-action and animated cartoons, and included: a short story by Sinclair Lewis; the antics of Edgar Bergen, Charlie McCarthy and Mortimer Snerd; the aphorisms of Jiminy Cricket; and Mickey Mouse, Donald Duck and Goofy in the "Happy Valley" sequence, better known as "Mickey and the Beanstalk." *Below:* a posed publicity still features the principals of the film.

A pall has descended on Happy Valley, for the magical Golden Harp that brings everyone good fortune has disappeared.

Mickey and his friends are starving, like everyone else in the Valley. Their last meal is a single slice of bread—to be divided evenly.

Poor Donald Duck! He stares with disbelief at his portion, which is so thin as to be transparent!

Such woebegone expressions on Goofy's and Donald's faces. But who can blame them, with such an unpalatable meal in front of them?

No, there aren't even any leftovers left over, Mickey.

The only thing left to do is to sell your cow, in hopes of getting some sustenance in return.

Vhat ho! Mickey returns with a fair trade—a box containing a single bean...

...it's not edible, but maybe it's magical...?

Doops! The bean falls through a crack in the floorboard, and Mickey stares forlornly into the blackness—unaware that germination is already taking place.

Fantastic! The bean sprouts into a mighty stalk, and our adventurous threesome mount an expedition upwards. They ascend to a wondrous land, with a magnificent castle in the distance.

Might as well head for the castle, and see who runs this burg....

When they arrive at the castle, they discover the Magic Harp, and promise that they will rescue her. But first, our hungry heroes must find some food....

Jnmindful of anything but the huge spread before them, Mickey and Donald and Goofy dive into the food, devouring everything with relish.

Goofy! Don't you know it's bad etiquette to eat peas with your knife?

Gawrsh! It's a real live Giant, who seems happy-go-lucky, if it weren't for his size!

He looks like one of those hunks who doesn't know his own strength.

It's suppertime, Giant-style—though he doesn't know about his uninvited guests.

Hmmmm! Something suspicious going on here....

"Ulp! Hiya, big boy," says Mickey as he pops out from his hiding place.

The Giant can't believe his eyes. What is this pipsqueak, a pimento?

As the Giant stares dumbfounded at our hero, Mickey decides to not stick around.

He makes a run for it. . . .

Cornered! "And where do you think you're going?"

Our heroes manage to find adequate hiding places.

The Giant is distracted by whatever it is he has in that chest.

But Donald and Goofy (hiding in a convenient keyhole) are distracted by their worry for Mickey. Where is he?

The Giant's prize possession is a hot Magic Harp, the same article that brought peace and contentment to Happy Valley.

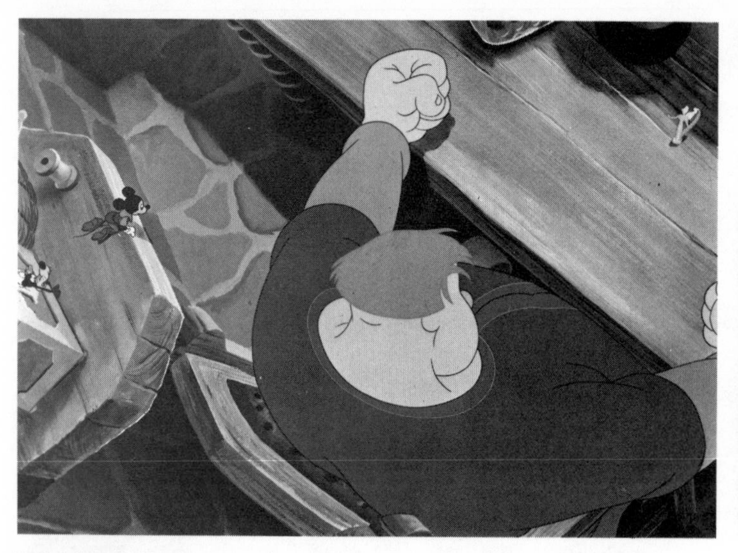

Our friends look down from above, as the Giant gloats over his treasure.

As the Giant takes a nap, the boys decide to rescue the Harp.

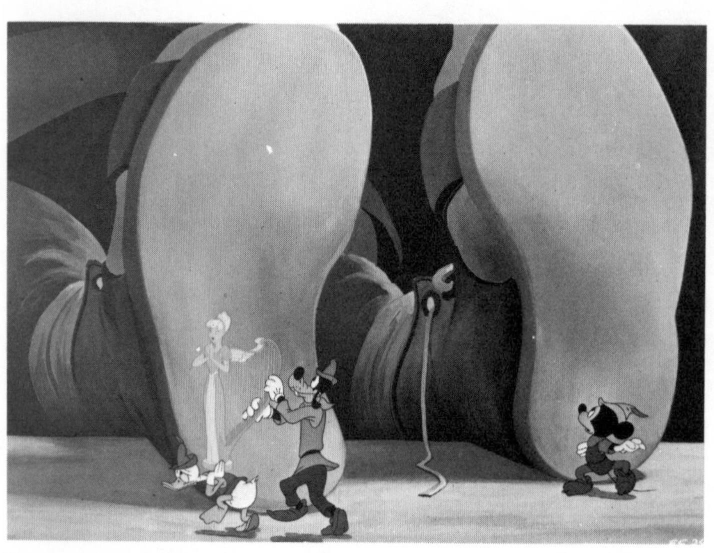

They make off with it on tiptoe, hoping not to wake the Giant.

When the Giant awakes, he discovers his loss, and confronts the Harp's rescuers: "Surprise!"

They get away, but before you know it, the Giant has almost caught up with Mickey.

EEK! But Mickey effects a narrow escape.

Mickey, Donald and Goofy manage to escape with the Magic Harp, in a pea pod boat....

Quickly, they clamber down the beanstalk with their rescued Magic Harp, and...

...begin sawing away at the beanstalk. A happy ending for everyone but the Giant!

Plutopia, 1951

While Mickey and Pluto are at a mountain resort, Pluto dreams of a utopian (read Plutopian) world where he is master of a household, with a cat for a butler. Every time he wants something, he nips the cat's tail. "Plutopia" was one of many cartoons produced in the Forties and Fifties where Mickey took a subsidiary role to Pluto. This trend had begun in the late Thirties when the cartoon situations were shared by Mickey, Donald and Goofy—such as "Mickey's Service Station" or "Clock Cleaners."

Pluto's Christmas Tree, 1952

Mickey chops down a tree for Christmas, not knowing that it is the home of Chip and Dale. When the tree is set up and decorated, Pluto tries unsuccessfully to warn Mickey of the interlopers. He manages to destroy the tree in his mad chase, but in the end, all sing carols except Pluto, who has a "Do Not Open Until Christmas" sticker over his mouth.

The Mickey Mouse Club, 1955–1958

The Mickey Mouse Club became a national phenomenon immediately upon its release. The combination of the Disney name, cartoons, and a talented group of energetic young performers was irresistable to the millions of young viewers. Each day, the show opened with a flashing billboard, "Walt Disney and Mickey Mouse present the Mickey Mouse Club." Mickey would appear in full bandleader's regalia, conducting all his cartoon friends in a rousing chorus of "Who's the leader of the club that's made for you and me? M-I-C-K-E-Y M-O-U-S-E!"

Walt Disney
and
MICKEY
MOUSE

Present
the...

Mickey Mouse
CLUB

BOBBY
JIMMIE
MARGENE
EILEEN
LONNIE
LARRY
CHERYL
TOMMY
DARLENE
SHARON
SHERRY
CUBBY

Monday

Tuesday

Wednesday

Thursday

The Mickey Mouse Club had five theme days: Monday was Fun with Music Day; Tuesday was Guest Star Day; Wednesday was Anything Can Happen Day; Thursday was Circus Day; Friday was Talent Roundup Day. Mickey would appear in costume to introduce the activities.

Friday

The musical numbers were always elaborately staged, and costumes for the Mousekeeters ranged from their Mouse Club uniforms to those of hoboes, cats, angels, and even Swiss clock figurines.

Clockwise, from upper left: Jimmie Dodd, singer and songwriter and Mouseketeer, with Annette Funicello, Doreen Tracy, and Bobby Burgess. *Opposite page:* Each day featured a Disney cartoon, drawn from the Club's "Treasure Mine."

MICKEY MOUSE TREASURE MINE
"KLONDIKE KID"

Mickey's wonderful vintage cartoons were a frequent bonus on the show.

"The Chain Gang," 1930, with Pegleg Pete as the brutal prison guard.

"Grocery Boy," 1932, with Minnie Mouse.

"On Ice," 1935.

"Mickey's Polo Team," 1936, featured a cast of Hollywood characters. Aside from the Big Bad Wolf and Goofy, Oliver Hardy (astride a lookalike horse!) and a slice of Stan Laurel are evident in this picture.

"Mickey's Grand Opera," 1936, with Clarabelle the Cow.

"Alpine Climbers," 1936.

The Club featured serials such as "Spin and Marty," featuring Tim Considine and David Stollery; "Corky and White Shadow," with Darlene Gillespie; "Annette," with Roberta Shore, Considine, and Annette Funicello; and "The Hardy Boys," with Tommy Kirk, Florenz Ames, and Tim Considine.

Fridays were Talent Roundup Days, where not only the Mouseketeers but special guests showed off what they could do. Guests received a certificate upon performing, and were welcomed as honorary Mouseketeers. *Below, opposite page:* Roy Williams, who was a Disney cartoonist, was chosen by chance to be a Mooseketeer. He often got to demonstrate the art of cartooning on the show.

SPECIAL TALENT AWARD

WHEREAS THE RECIPIENT HAS DEMONSTRATED OUTSTANDING ABILITY AS A CONTESTANT IN THE MICKEY MOUSE CLUB NATIONAL "TALENT ROUNDUP", THIS SPECIAL TALENT AWARD CERTIFICATE IS HEREBY OFFICIALLY CONFERRED.

MICKEY MOUSE CLUB

JOINT SPONSORS
THE BROADWAY—SOUTHERN CALIFORNIA
STATION KABC-TV

SIGNED... Walt Disney
CHIEF MARSHAL
MICKEY MOUSE CLUB

MOUSEGETAR-JR.

ıe Mickey Mouse Club inspired a host of merchandise, including the Mousegetar Jr. *pposite page*), the Mousears and shirt, and the Mickey Mouse Bandleader Outfit (*below*).

Musical numbers were always prevalent. *Above:* The Mouseketeers sing their parting song, "Now it's time to say goodbye to all our company . . ."

Opposite: Walt Disney and producer Bill Walsh on the set.

Disneyland, 1955

Though he had mulled over the idea of an alternative to amusement parks for nearly twenty years, his brainchild—Disneyland—did not open until July 1955. Situated on 160 acres of former orange groves, the Disneyland theme park was built on a foundation of years of motic picture knowhow. There is an extraordinary continuity to the park, which is most evident as visitors are led from one locale to another (Adventureland, Frontierland, Fantasyland, Tomorrowland), very much in the fashion that a camera will travel into and through a scene. Walt Disney did not forget who it was who helped him to fame and for tune—so Mickey Mouse is very evident at Disneyland.

GIFTS

WALT DISNEY'S
Disneyland

Disneyland

On December 15, 1966, Walt Disney died of acute circulatory collapse, following surgery one month earlier. *Above:* The Paris *Match* marked Disney's passing with this evocative portrait of Mickey. Disney's death marked the end of one kind of era at the Studio, and in all the other Disney enterprises. But they all continue to run smoothly without his guidance, though it's certain they all miss his personal dedication.

Walt Disney World, 1971

Following the enormous success of Disneyland, Walt Disney began thinking of a similar enterprise for East Coast travelers. Florida, with its healthy tourist seasons and year-round pleasant weather, offered a natural setting. Acreage for Walt Disney World was quietly acquired, with Disney supervising the overall operation. Disney hoped to avoid the problems he encountered with the theme park in Anaheim; it is unfortunate that he did not live long enough to see the Florida operation, for he would have been pleased. His brother Roy opened the park in October, 1971. Mickey Mouse again became a prominent presence.

FLY EASTERN
YOUR WINGS TO THE FAMILY VACATION KINGDOM
Walt Disney World
EASTERN
THE OFFICIAL AIRLINE OF
Walt Disney World

JOIN MICKEY
and see the world

ARMED FORCES DAYS • MAY 21 - JUNE 5

Walt Disney World

Above: Roy Disney opens the park during dedication ceremonies in October 1971. *Below left:* Olympic star Olga Korbut is guided around the park by Mickey. *Below right:* Jimmy Carter was only one of many dignitaries to visit Walt Disney World.

Above: A sophisticated computer-controlled system called Audio-Animatronics governs this light-hearted attraction, "Mickey's Revue."

The New Mickey Mouse Club, 1977

Over twenty years after the original Mickey Mouse Club aired in 1955, a new version appeared in January 1977. Featuring twelve new Mouseketeers who ranged in age from eight to fourteen, the new club continued the format of theme days. Disney's timeless cartoons appeared daily, as did new Mickey Mouse animation. The production stressed an air of colorful, contemporary, and energetic fun, with music of a decidedly "rock" nature.

ouse Club alumni Annette Funicello and Tim Considine returned to visit the new Mouseketeers.

The Studio produced new animation of Mickey Mouse for his new club.
Each day, Mickey appeared to introduce the show's activities.

The New Mickey Mouse Club"
eatured Mickey's cartoons,
uch as "Mickey's Delayed Date,"
947 *(top)*; "Mickey Down Under,"
948 *(center)*; and "The Little
Vhirlwind," 1941 *(bottom)*.

The Wardrobe Manager for "The New Mickey Mouse Club" was kept busy— for the new Mouseketeers appeared in many imaginative costumes.

Daily Gags, 1960's & 1970's

The Mickey Mouse Daily Gags included here were written at different times by: Bill Walsh, Roy Williams, and Del Connell, and drawn by Floyd Gottfredson. The series reaches an average of 1.8 million Americans, and 3.75 million in foreign markets.

■ ■ ■

■ ■ ■

WHEW!
Distributed by King Features Syndicate.

MORTY.. I'VE TOLD YOU NOT TO SMELL UP THE HOUSE WITH THAT CHEMISTRY SET!

WRETCH! I WAS COOKING YOU A SURPRISE DINNER!
© 1960 Walt Disney Productions World Rights Reserved
WALT DISNEY
8-15

© 1970 Walt Disney Productions World Rights Reserved
C'MON IN, MICKEY!
IS IT SAFE?
BEWARE OF WATCHDOG

SURE! MY NEW DOG WON'T BOTHER YOU...

RIGHT NOW HE'S ONLY INTERESTED IN ME!
Distributed by King Features Syndicate.
3-24

I DIDN'T KNOW YOU HAD A BOWLING BALL, GOOFY!
© 1970 Walt Disney Productions World Rights Reserved

Distributed by King Features Syndicate.
I BOUGHT IT LAST NIGHT AT THUH BOWLING ALLEY...

HAD TO — COULDN'T GET MUH THUMB OUT!
3 28

Copyright © 1974 Walt Disney Productions World Rights Reserved
Grand OPENING
KUNG FU

WHAT'S WRONG, GOOFY?

I THOUGHT THAT WAS A NEW CHINESE RESTAURANT!
Distributed by King Features Syndicate.
12-18

Copyright © 1975
Walt Disney Productions
World Rights Reserved

THE PET SHOP HAD A GOING-OUT-OF-BUSINESS SALE!
10-27 Distributed by King Features Syndicate.

THAT'S IT, MORTY— GENTLEMEN WALK ON THE OUTSIDE!

!
© 1969
Walt Disney Productions
World Rights Reserved

Distributed by King Features Syndicate.
2-7

■ ■ ■

OH! MY TEA LEAVES SAY I'M GOING TO MEET A HANDSOME STRANGER!
TEA
Distributed by King Features Syndicate.

EEOOEEEE
I'LL DRIVE AROUND SO WE CAN FIND EACH OTHER!
© 1970
Walt Disney Productions
World Rights Reserved

I'M SWITCHING TO COFFEE, HANDSOME!
?
3-27
P.D.

■ ■ ■

© 1960
Walt Disney Productions
World Rights Reserved

Distributed by King Features Syndicate.
AUCTION WAREHOUSE
Special
AUCTION
MUNICIPAL
EQUIPMENT
!

IT'S A LITTLE SLOW.. BUT I GET RESPECT!
WALT DISNEY
8-16
!
MUNICIPAL
WATER
TRUCK
!

Copyright © 1974
Walt Disney Productions
World Rights Reserved
YOU CAN USE THIS HOLE, MICKEY! I'VE CAUGHT MUH LIMIT!

IT'S SO COLD OUT— HOW COME YOU'RE STILL SITTING AROUND?

Distributed by King Features Syndicate.
MUH BOOTS ARE FROZEN TO THUH ICE!
12/20

■ ■ ■

HERE WE ARE! ECHO LAKE!
HELLO, THERE!
ECHO LAKE

HELLO, THERE!
THERE'S THUH ECHO!
© 1960
Walt Disney Productions
World Rights Reserved

Distributed by King Features Syndicate.
TWENTY-FIVE DOLLARS APIECE FOR YOUR LICENSES, PLEASE!
WALT DISNEY
8-20

■ ■ ■

I THINK I'LL QUIT SCHOOL AND GET A JOB!

TOO MUCH HOMEWORK, EH?
NO...

Distributed by King Features Syndicate.
TOO LITTLE ALLOWANCE!
Copyright © 1974
Walt Disney Productions
World Rights Reserved
12-19

■ ■ ■

THOSE KIDS PLAYING BASEBALL! AND ME WITH A HEADACHE!
HIT IT, MORTY! YAY!
CRACK!

© 1960
Walt Disney Productions
World Rights Reserved

YOUR UNCA MICKEY'S KEEN! DIDN'T COMPLAIN ABOUT US KNOCKIN' THE BALL IN HERE!
Distributed by King Features Syndicate.
WALT DISNEY
8-17

The Phenomenon Continues, 1970's

Mickey Mouse and his friends continue to appear on toys and other children's items, as his fiftieth birthday approaches. The merchandising operation is now carried on through the Disney Burbank office, as they license manufacturers to produce lunch boxes, Mickey-in-the-Boxes, dolls, clothing, poster books, calendars, pencil boxes, etc. One nice trend is the reissuing of character merchandise from the Thirties—facsimile comic books and coloring books particularly.

Above: A commemorative plate celebrates the American Bicentennial, á la Disney. *Opposite page:* Disney merchandise may be had in plastic *(above)* or pewter *(below)*.

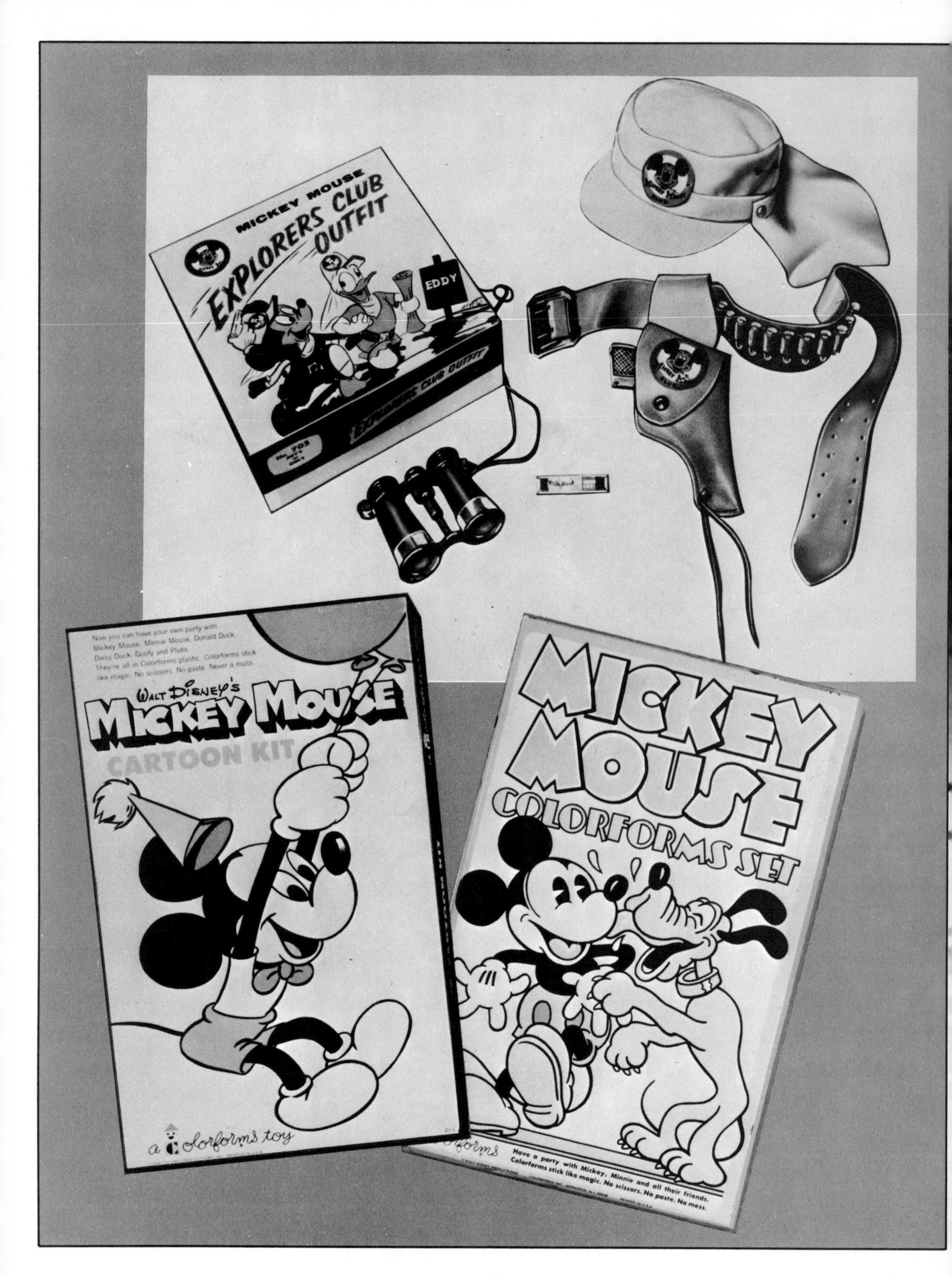
MICKEY MOUSE
EXPLORERS CLUB OUTFIT
EDDY
EXPLORERS CLUB OUTFIT
Now you can have your own party with
Mickey Mouse, Minnie Mouse, Donald Duck,
Daisy Duck, Goofy and Pluto.
They're all in Colorforms plastic. Colorforms stick
like magic. No scissors. No paste. Never a muss.
WALT DISNEY'S
MICKEY MOUSE
CARTOON KIT
a Colorforms toy
MICKEY MOUSE
COLORFORMS SET
Have a party with Mickey, Minnie and all their friends.
Colorforms stick like magic. No scissors. No paste. No mess.

CARRO
IMPROVED CHANTENAY
RADIS
EARLY SCARLET
CUCUMBE
MARKETER
PUMPK
LETTUCE
BLACK SEEDED SIMPSON
Net Wt.
1.5 g.
59¢
WALT DISNEY WONDERFUL WORLD OF GARDENING
MICKEY MOUSE
POP-UP
Play Set
A three-dimensional Pop-Up party
with funny hats, refreshments
and all the trimmings
in Colorforms magic plastic.
a Colorforms activity toy

Mickey Mouse Filmography

Mickey appeared in many other Disney cartoon shorts, but in minor roles.

1928 Plane Crazy
Gallopin' Gaucho
Steamboat Willie

1929 The Barn Dance
The Opry House
When the Cat's Away
The Barnyard Battle
The Plow Boy
The Karnival Kid
Mickey's Follies
Mickey's Choo-Choo
The Jazz Fool
Jungle Rhythm
The Haunted House
Wild Waves

1930 Just Mickey
The Barnyard Concert
The Cactus Kid
The Fire Fighters
The Shindig
The Chain Gang
The Gorilla Mystery
The Picnic
Pioneer Days

1931 The Birthday Party
Traffic Troubles
The Castaway
The Moose Hunt
The Delivery Boy
Mickey Steps Out
Blue Rhythm
Fishin' Around
The Barnyard Broadcast
The Beach Party
Mickey Cuts Up
Mickey's Orphans

1932 The Duck Hunt
The Grocery Boy
The Mad Dog
Barnyard Olympics
Mickey's Revue
Musical Farmer
Mickey in Arabia
Mickey's Nightmare
Trader Mickey
The Whoopee Party
Touchdown Mickey
The Wayward Canary
The Klondike Kid
Mickey's Good Deed

1933 Building a Building
The Mad Doctor
Mickey's Pal Pluto
Mickey's Mellerdrammer

Ye Olden Days
The Mail Pilot
Mickey's Mechanical Man
Mickey's Gala Premier
Puppy Love
The Steeple-Chase
The Pet Store
Giantland

1934 Camping Out
Shanghaied
Playful Pluto
Mickey's Steam-Roller
Gulliver Mickey
Orphans' Benefit
Mickey Plays Papa
The Dognapper
Two-Gun Mickey

1935 Mickey's Man Friday
Mickey's Service Station
Mickey's Kangaroo
The Band Concert
Mickey's Garden
Mickey's Fire Brigade
Pluto's Judgement Day
On Ice

1936 Mickey's Grand Opera
Mickey's Polo Team
Orphans' Picnic
Mickey's Rival
Thru the Mirror
Moving Day
Alpine Climbers
Mickey's Circus
Mickey's Elephant

1937 The Worm Turns
Magician Mickey
Moose Hunters
Mickey's Amateurs
Lonesome Ghosts
Clock Cleaners
Hawaiian Holiday

1938 Boat Builders
Mickey's Trailer
Brave Little Tailor
The Whalers
Mickey's Parrot

1939 Society Dog Show
The Pointer

1940 Tugboat Mickey
Pluto's Dream House
Mr. Mouse Takes a Trip
The Sorcerer's Apprentice
Orphans' Benefit (*remake*)

1941 The Little Whirlwind
The Nifty Nineties

1942 Mickey's Birthday Party
Symphony Hour

1947 Mickey's Delayed Date
Mickey and the Beanstalk

1948 Mickey and the Seal
Mickey Down Under

1951 Plutopia
R'coon Dawg

1952 Pluto's Party
Pluto's Christmas Tree

1953 The Simple Things

Bibliography

Books

Arseni, Ercole. *Walt Disney's Magic Moments.* Mondadori, 1973.

Feild, R.D. *The Art of Walt Disney.* Macmillan, 1942.

Finch, Christopher, *The Art of Walt Disney.* Abrams, 1973.

Jacobs, Lewis. *Introduction to the Art of the Movies.* Noonday, 1960.

Keller, Keith. *The Mickey Mouse Club Scrapbook.* Grosset and Dunlap, 1975.

Maltin, Leonard. *The Disney Films.* Crown, 1973.

Miller, Diane Disney (As told to Pete Martin). *The Story of Walt Disney.* Holt, 1957.

Munsey, Cecil. *Disneyana: Walt Disney Collectibles.* Hawthorne, 1974.

Schickel, Richard. *The Disney Version.* Avon, 1969.

Taylor, Deems. *Walt Disney's Fantasia.* Simon and Schuster, 1940.

Thomas, Bob. *Walt Disney: An American Original.* Simon and Schuster, 1976.

Articles

Birmingham, Stephen. "The Greatest One Man Show on Earth." *McCall's,* July, 1964.

Bright, John. "Disney's Fantasy Empire." *The Nation,* Mar. 6, 1967.

Churchill, Douglas. "Now Mickey Mouse Enters Art's Temple." *The New York Times Magazine,* June 3, 1934.

Crowther, Bosley. "The Dream Merchant." *The New York Times,* Dec. 16, 1966.

Davidson, Bill. "The Fantastic Walt Disney." *The Saturday Evening Post,* Nov. 7, 1964.

Forster, E.M. "Mickey and Minnie." The London *Spectator,* Jan. 19, 1934.

Johnston, Alva. "Mickey Mouse." *Woman's Home Companion,* July 1934.

Paris Match. "Farewell to Walt Disney." Dec. 24, 1966.

Russel, Herbert. "Of L'Affaire Mickey Mouse." *The New York Times Magazine,* Dec. 26, 1937.

Seldes, Gilbert. "No Art, Mr. Disney?" *Esquire,* Sept. 1937.

"I hope we never lose sight of one fact . . .
that this was all started by a Mouse."
—Walt Disney